ADDISON-WESLEY TOEIC®

TOEIC® Preparation Workbook

LIN LOUGHEED

ADDISON-WESLEY PUBLISHERS JAPAN LTD.

Tokyo • Reading, Massachusetts • Menlo Park, California • New York • Don Mills, Ontario
Workingham, England • Amsterdam • Bonn • Sydney • Singapore • Madrid • San Juan

TOEIC is a registered trademark of Educational Testing Service. However, there is no connection between this publisher and Educational Testing Service.

A publication of the World Language Division

Production: Karen Edmonds
Production Assistants: Lisa Schiffgens, Helen Papp
Additional Writing: D. Kennedy

Line drawings from Click Art ® Business Images, EPS Business Art, Personal Graphics and Business Cartoons by T/Maker Company. All rights reserved.

TOEIC® is a registered trademark of Educational Testing Service and used by the permission of Educational Testing Service, the copyright owner. However, all information within this text is provided in its entirety by Addison-Wesley Publishers. No endorsement of this publication by Educational Testing Service should be inferred.

Copyright © 1992 by Addison-Wesley Publishers in Japan, Ltd. All rights reserved. No part of this publication may be reproduced, stored in a retrieval system, or transmitted in any form or by any means, electronic, mechanical, photocopying, recording, or otherwise, without the prior written permission of the publisher.

Printed in Japan

ISBN 0-201-56236-7

2 3 4 5 6 7 8 9 10-J-96 95 94 93 92

Contents

How to Use This Book, iv

1	**Geography**, 1
2	**The Weather**, 5
3	**The City**, 9
4	**General Business Terms**, 13
5	**Types of Businesses**, 17
6	**Restaurants**, 21
7	**Office Terms**, 25
8	**Construction**, 29
9	**Entertaining**, 33
10	**Teaching**, 37
11	**Medicine**, 41
12	**Hotel Service**, 45
13	**Gardening and Farming**, 49
14	**The Gas Station**, 53
15	**The Military**, 57
16	**The Police and the Law**, 61
17	**Artists**, 65
18	**Banks**, 69
19	**Travel**, 73
20	**Trains**, 77
21	**Cars**, 81
22	**Roads**, 85
23	**The Body**, 89
24	**Clothes**, 93
25	**Housework**, 97
26	**The Living Room**, 101
27	**The Kitchen**, 105
28	**The Post Office**, 109
29	**Food**, 113
30	**Money**, 117

Answer Key, 121

How to Use This Book

The TOEIC® Preparation Workbook is designed to help you improve your vocabulary and reading skills. This workbook is divided into 30 chapters. Each chapter covers topics from normal, everyday life with words associated with the topic.

Each chapter is divided into three sections: Words to Know, Word Practice, and Reading Practice.

Words to Know
The Words to Know vocabulary list may contain some words you already know. You should concentrate on the words that are new to you.

Word Practice
Each word in the vocabulary list is used in one of the activities in the Word Practice section. The activities will teach you how to quickly recognize the words from their spelling patterns, how to categorize them, and how to define and use them.

Reading Practice
The Reading Practice section has three types of questions similar to those on the TOEIC test: Error Recognition, Paragraph Comprehension, Conversation Comprehension.

The underlined words in the Error Recognition section may contain errors of the following grammatical types:

Word Families	Two-Word Verbs
Prepositions	Articles
Conjunctions	Pronouns
Adverbs of Frequency	Subject-Verb Agreement
Causative Verbs	Modal Auxiliaries
Conditional Sentences	Adjective Comparisons
Verb Tense	Gerunds and Infinitives

You do not need to start with Chapter One. You may start anywhere in the workbook and study only those chapters where you need to improve your vocabulary.

You should write your answers directly in the book and compare your answer with the answers given in the Answer Key. The Answer Key is in the back of the book.

1 GEOGRAPHY

WORDS TO KNOW

Antarctic Circle	ground	north	sea
Arctic Circle	gulf	North Pole	shore
coast	hill	ocean	south
earth	island	peninsula	South Pole
east	lake	plain	stream
Equator	land	plateau	valley
field	map	pond	waterfall
forest	mountain	river	west
globe	mountain range	river bank	woods

WORD PRACTICE

1. Label the parts of the globe.

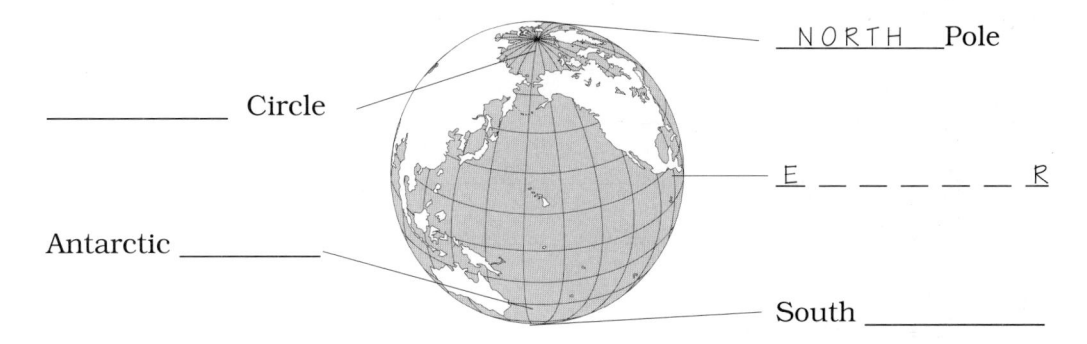

- _NORTH_ Pole
- _____ Circle
- E _ _ _ _ _ R
- Antarctic _____
- South _____

2. Circle the correct word.

1. The Sahara and the Mohave are examples of (mountains / (deserts)).

2. The Nile and Amazon are examples of (oceans / rivers).

3. Everest and Fuji are examples of (mountains / seas).

4. The Atlantic and the Pacific are examples of (continents / oceans).

5. Japan and Hawaii are examples of (islands / peninsulas).

6. Niagara and Victoria are examples of (waterfalls / ponds).

7. The Urals and Andes are examples of (mountain ranges / creeks).

3. Write the geographic term under the appropriate label.

	WATER	LAND
1. ocean	OCEAN	
2. mountain		MOUNTAIN
3. hill		
4. river		
5. shore		
6. pond		
7. valley		
8. creek		
9. stream		
10. peninsula		
11. plateau		
12. sea		
13. surf		
14. continent		
15. lake		
16. bay		

4. Complete the following sentences.

1. A farmer plants wheat in the F I E L D .
2. The flood waters ran over the R _ V _ _ B _ _ _ .
3. Early settlers traveled across the rich fertile P _ _ _ N S .
4. The farm animals drink water from the P _ _ D .
5. Many people work and live on both the Atlantic and the Pacific C _ _ _ T S .
6. The F _ _ _ _ T fires destroyed acres of trees.
7. The E _ _ _ _ is the third planet from the sun.
8. Children learn about the world by studying G _ _ _ _ S and M _ _ _ .

2

5. Complete the directions on the compass.

North

4. _____

West

1. _____

3. _____

Northeast

Southeast

2. _____

READING PRACTICE

1. Which underlined word is incorrect? Circle the letter.

> **GRAMMAR TO KNOW:**
> prepositions   pronouns
> subject-verb agreement   verb tense

1. The small stream <u>at</u> the top of the mountain <u>flow</u> into a <u>large</u> river.
               A   (B)   C

2. The <u>North</u> Pole <u>lie</u> inside <u>the</u> Arctic Circle.
      A   B   C

3. We live <u>on</u> a peninsula, which <u>was</u> a narrow strip <u>of</u> land.
       A   B   C

4. The valley <u>are</u> surrounded by mountains <u>covered</u> <u>with</u> forests.
        A   B C

5. Tomorrow, Mr. Johnson <u>was</u> flying south of <u>the</u> equator <u>to</u> Rio.
                   A   B   C

6. These fish <u>is</u> too large to live <u>in</u> the lake, so they must live in <u>the</u> ocean.
        A   B   C

7. Look at a map <u>to</u> the bay and <u>count</u> the <u>number</u> of islands.
           A   B   C

8. When the American settlers <u>moved</u> west, <u>it</u> settled <u>on</u> the plain.
                          A   B   C

9. On <u>the</u> other side <u>from</u> that hill, there <u>is</u> a small swimming pond.
        A   B   C

10. The forest <u>at</u> the edge of the valley <u>have</u> many kinds <u>of</u> trees.
          A   B   C

2. Read the following conversation and answer the questions.

Man:	Where would you prefer to live? In the mountains or by the sea?
Woman:	I like the dry climate of the desert.
Man:	Not me. I prefer the woods and lakes.
Woman:	I like the quietness of a desert island.

1. What does the woman prefer?
   (A) The desert
   (B) The ocean
   (C) The mountains

2. What is common to a desert?
   (A) A dry climate
   (B) A lake
   (C) A sea

3. What does the man prefer?
   (A) The desert
   (B) The woods
   (C) The ocean

4. What kind of island is mentioned?
   (A) A mountainous island
   (B) An island in a lake
   (C) A desert island

3. Read the following paragraph and answer the questions.

> The Mississippi River begins in the Great Plains. It continues south and empties into the Gulf of Mexico. The Gulf of Mexico borders the eastern coast of Texas and the western shore of Florida. Florida is a peninsula. The Gulf is on its west and the Atlantic Ocean is on its east.

1. Where does the Mississippi River begin?
   (A) In the Great Plains
   (B) At the Gulf of Mexico
   (C) In Texas

2. Which direction does the Mississippi flow?
   (A) North
   (B) East
   (C) South

3. What is Florida?
   (A) A gulf
   (B) A peninsula
   (C) An ocean

4. What is east of Florida?
   (A) The Atlantic Ocean
   (B) The Gulf of Mexico
   (C) Texas

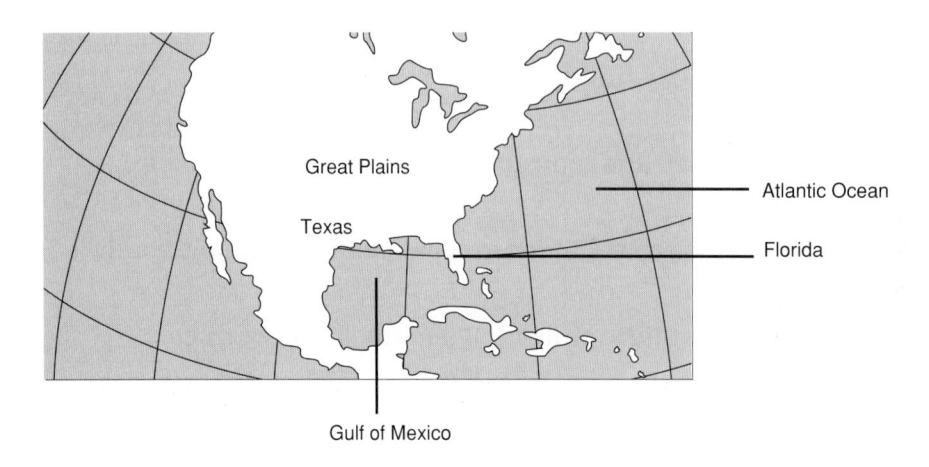

2 THE WEATHER

WORDS TO KNOW

breeze	earth	lightning	sun
clear	flood	rain	temperature
cloud	forecast	rainstorm	thunder
cold	freeze	sky	thunderstorm
cool	hot	snow	warm
drought	humid	snowstorm	wind
dry	ice	storm	windstorm

WORD PRACTICE

1. Draw a line to connect opposites.

    warm — cloudy
    dry — cool
    cold — humid
    clear — hot

2. Make a compound noun by adding the word *storm* to the following.

    rain   RAINSTORM

    thunder   _____

    wind   _____

    snow   _____

3. Cross out the word that does NOT belong.

1. cool   warm   ~~earth~~   temperature
2. ice   freeze   cold   hot
3. dry   drought   hot   snow
4. wind   breeze   sun   windstorm
5. thunder   lightning   sky   temperature

| Sunny | Cloudy | Stormy | Rainy |

5

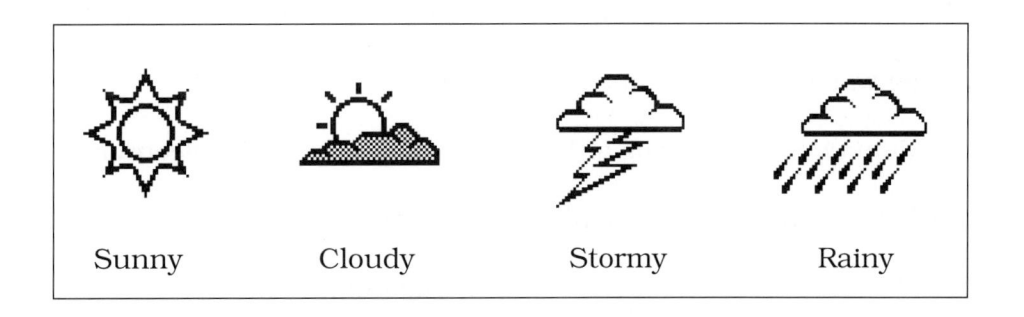

4. Make adjectives out of these words. Add -y.

NOUN	ADJECTIVE
wind	WINDY
cloud	_____
snow	_____
storm	_____
rain	_____

> **NOTE THESE DIFFERENCES:**
> | NOUN | ADJECTIVE |
> |---|---|
> | ice | icy |
> | sun | sunny |
> | breeze | breezy |

5. Complete these sentences with an adjective.

1. There are many <u>clouds</u> in the sky. It's a C L O U D Y day.
2. The <u>winds</u> are very strong. It's a _____ day.
3. Five inches of <u>snow</u> will fall. It will be a _____ day.
4. The forecast calls for rain<u>storms</u>. It will be _____ .
5. The <u>breezes</u> will blow from the south. It will be a _____ morning.
6. The <u>rain</u> will continue until 6 p.m. It will be a _____ day.
7. After the <u>ice</u> storm, the roads will be _____ .
8. The <u>sun</u> will rise at 5:42 a.m., and the day will be _____ .

6. Circle the correct word.

1. The ((sky)/ breeze) is sunny and blue.
2. The noise from the (thunderstorm/cloud) frightened the children.
3. When water (freezes/runs), ice is formed.
4. (Lightning/Snow) during a thunderstorm is caused by electricity.
5. The (temperature/wind) is above 20 degrees Celsius.
6. The lack of rain is bad for the (earth/thunder).

Reading Practice

1. Which underlined word is incorrect? Circle the letter.

> **GRAMMAR TO KNOW:**
> adjectives   articles
> prepositions   subject-verb agreement

1. Tomorrow <u>the</u> weather will <u>be</u> hot and <u>humidity</u>.
              A   B   Ⓒ

2. <u>The</u> roads <u>was</u> <u>icy</u> after the storm.
     A   B C

3. <u>There</u> were few <u>clouds</u> <u>on</u> the sky.
     A   B   C

4. The <u>temperature</u> today <u>is</u> as <u>higher</u> as yesterday.
         A   B   C

5. <u>The</u> thunder <u>usually</u> <u>follows</u> lightning.
     A   B   C

6. <u>There</u> <u>were</u> a <u>cool</u>, pleasant breeze this afternoon.
     A   B   C

7. The earth's temperature <u>are</u> raised <u>by</u> the heat <u>of</u> the sun.
                           A   B   C

8. <u>The</u> thunderstorms <u>are</u> caused by warm air <u>meeting</u> cold air.
     A   B   C

9. Yesterday's snowstorm <u>put</u> four inches <u>in</u> snow <u>on</u> the ground.
                     A   B   C

10. In January, the temperature often <u>goes</u> below freezing and the sky is often
                                          A

    <u>covered</u> with <u>the</u> clouds.
      B   C

RAIN EXPRESSIONS

The following expressions mean "It's raining a lot":

1. It's raining cats and dogs.
2. It's coming down in buckets.
3. It's pouring.
4. It's raining really hard.

2. Read the following paragraph and answer the following questions.

> The lack of rain in the Southwest is causing a drought. However, in the Northeast the rainstorms are causing floods. In the Northwest, weather is normal.

1. Where is there no rain?
   - (A) In the Northeast
   - (B) In the Southwest
   - (C) In the Northwest

2. What causes a drought?
   - (A) Lack of rain
   - (B) Rainstorms
   - (C) Farmers

3. What causes floods?
   - (A) Lack of rain
   - (B) Rainstorms
   - (C) Droughts

4. Where are there floods?
   - (A) In the Northeast
   - (B) In the Southwest
   - (C) In the Northwest

3. Read the following weather report and answer the questions.

> This afternoon the weather will be hot and humid with the temperature above 40 degrees Celsius. This evening we will have thunderstorms with the possibility of 2-3 inches of rain. By morning the sky will be clear and tomorrow's weather will be sunny and breezy.

1. What is this afternoon's weather?
   - (A) Hot and humid
   - (B) Cool and dry
   - (C) Warm and breezy

2. When will the thunderstorms begin?
   - (A) Sometime this afternoon
   - (B) In the evening
   - (C) Tomorrow morning

3. How much rain is predicted?
   - (A) 40 inches
   - (B) 23 inches
   - (C) 2-3 inches

4. What is tomorrow's forecast?
   - (A) Cold and breezy
   - (B) Sunny and humid
   - (C) Clear and sunny

3 THE CITY

WORDS TO KNOW

alley	drive	museum	stadium
apartment house	entrance	newspaper stand	stop sign
boulevard	fire station	office building	store
building	freeway	opera house	street
bus stop	highway	parking lot	street light
city hall	hospital	parking meter	street sign
concert hall	hotel	phone booth	suburb
crosswalk	house	police station	subway
curb	lane	road	station
downtown	movie theater	sidewalk	traffic light

WORD PRACTICE

1. Circle the appropriate word.

1. This light turns green, red or yellow. It tells traffic when to stop or go.
   It is a (*traffic light* / *street light*).

2. This light comes on at night. It helps people see when it's dark.
   It is a (*traffic light* / *street light*).

3. This sign is red. It is shaped like this: 🛑 Cars stop at this sign.
   It is a (*stop sign* / *street sign*).

4. This sign is usually green. It is shaped like this: ▬ This sign helps people find a street.
   It is a (*stop sign* / *street sign*).

5. I want to take an underground train.
   I should wait at a (*bus stop* / *subway station*).

6. I want to take the crosstown bus.
   I should wait at a (*bus stop* / *subway station*).

7. I want to make a phone call.
   I should go to a (*newspaper stand* / *telephone booth*).

8. I want to buy a newspaper.
   I should go to a (*newspaper stand* / *telephone booth*).

9

2. Write the words for types of buildings.

1. Workers work here:

    <u>O</u> <u>F</u> <u>F</u> <u>I</u> <u>C</u> <u>E</u> building

2. This is a city government building:

    <u>C</u> __ __ __   <u>H</u> __ __ __

3. A place to watch a movie:

    <u>M</u> __ __ __ __   __ __ __ __ __ __

4. A place where many people live:

    <u>A</u> __ __ __ __ __ __ __   <u>H</u> __ __ __ __

5. A place to listen to a symphony:

    <u>C</u> <u>O</u> __ __ __ __ __   <u>H</u> __ __ __

6. A place to see exhibitions:

    <u>M</u> <u>U</u> __ __ __ __

7. A theater for opera:

    <u>O</u> <u>P</u> __ __ __   <u>H</u> __ __ __ __

8. A place for sick people:

    <u>H</u> __ __ __ __ __ __

9. Travelers sleep here:

    <u>H</u> __ <u>T</u> __ __

3. Write the words for types of roads.

1. <u>S</u> <u>T</u> <u>R</u> <u>E</u> <u>E</u> <u>T</u>   5. <u>F</u> __ __ __ __ __ __
2. <u>R</u> __ __ __   6. <u>L</u> __ __ __ __
3. <u>H</u> __ __ __ __ __ __   7. <u>D</u> __ __ __ __
4. <u>A</u> __ __ __ __   8. <u>B</u> __ __ __ __ __ __ __

4. Complete the following paragraph.

Crossing the Street

   The pedestrians waited on the <u>S</u> __ __ __ <u>W</u> __ __ __ for the traffic light to change. When the sign across the street said "WALK," they stepped off the <u>C</u> __ __ __ and walked across the busy street in the <u>C</u> __ __ __ __ <u>W</u> __ __ __.

5. Complete the following paragraph.

Parking

John drove into the city. He didn't have enough change for a
P _ _ _ _ _ _ _   M _ _ _ _ so he looked for a
P _ _ _ _ _ _ _   L _ _ , but they were all full. "Next time,
I'll take the bus," he thought.

READING PRACTICE

1. Which underlined word is incorrect? Circle the letter.

> **GRAMMAR TO KNOW:**
> conjunctions   gerunds
> prepositions   verb tense

1. Each morning she waits <u>at</u> the bus stop <u>for</u> go <u>to</u> work downtown.
                              A   (B) C

2. When the man <u>crossing</u> the street, he <u>did</u> not notice that the traffic light
                 A   B
<u>had turned</u> red.
    C

3. Our office building <u>has</u> a store <u>but</u> a movie theater <u>on</u> the first two floors.
                        A   B   C

4. I do not <u>drive</u> to work. It is too expensive to <u>parking</u> <u>in</u> a parking lot.
        A   B C

5. <u>On</u> Saturday, let's <u>going</u> <u>to</u> the stadium to see a baseball game.
   A   B C

6. <u>The</u> parking meter next <u>of</u> the telephone booths <u>is</u> out of order.
   A   B   C

7. When guests <u>came</u> to the city to visit <u>me,</u> <u>they</u> always stay at a hotel.
              A   B C

8. Traffic <u>at</u> the freeway this morning was <u>moving</u> <u>slowly</u>.
      A   B C

9. <u>Got</u> into the right lane, turn <u>at</u> the next road <u>and</u> you'll see City Hall.
  A   B   C

10. The <u>riders</u> left <u>the</u> subway station <u>while</u> walked to the museum.
       A   B   C

2. Read the following paragraph and answer the questions.

> The Department of Streets and Highways announced today that a new highway connecting downtown and the suburban airport will be built. The 10-mile highway will be six lanes wide. The highway will replace Adams Boulevard which in recent years has often been congested.

1. What will be built?
   (A) A new highway
   (B) An airport
   (C) A new boulevard

2. Where is the airport?
   (A) Downtown
   (B) In the suburbs
   (C) 6 miles away

3. How wide will the highway be?
   (A) 6 miles
   (B) 6 lanes
   (C) 10 miles

4. What has been the problem with Adams Boulevard?
   (A) It's often congested.
   (B) It's not long enough.
   (C) It's not wide enough.

3. Read the following paragraph and answer the questions.

> The Center for Urban Living opens today. The Center offers a unique combination of residential, recreational and professional spaces. The Center will house apartments, city government offices, a theater, a concert hall, a grocery store, a stadium and a museum. The Center is located on major bus and subway lines. Parking is available in the Center's underground lots.

1. Where is the Center?
   (A) In an urban area
   (B) In the suburbs
   (C) In the country

2. Which is NOT found in the Center?
   (A) Apartments
   (B) A museum
   (C) A hospital

3. How can you reach the Center?
   (A) By subway
   (B) By plane
   (C) By boat

4. Where can you park at the Center?
   (A) Behind the stadium
   (B) In underground lots
   (C) On the roof

This view of a city is called its "skyline."

4 GENERAL BUSINESS TERMS

WORDS TO KNOW

bookcase	envelope	out-box	stapler
boss	fax machine	operator	supplies
calculator	file	paper clip	telephone
calendar	file cabinet	photocopier	typist
computer	in-box	receptionist	typewriter
desk	intercom	secretary	wastepaper basket
document	message	shorthand	word processor

WORD PRACTICE

1. Write the noun form for each of the following verbs.

1. compute   <u>COMPUTER</u>
2. operate   _____
3. type   _____
4. photocopy   _____
5. staple   _____

2. Write the words for machines used in an office.

1. A <u>T E L E P H O N E</u> is used to call clients.
2. A <u>C</u> _ _ <u>C</u> _ _ _ _ _ _ is used to add numbers.
3. A <u>C</u> _ _ <u>P</u> _ _ _ <u>R</u> is used to maintain records.
4. A <u>S</u> _ _ <u>P</u> _ _ <u>R</u> is used to attach papers together.
5. A <u>P</u> _ _ <u>T</u> _ _ _ _ _ _ is used to make copies.
6. A <u>W</u> _ _ <u>D</u>   <u>P</u> _ _ _ _ _ _ _ <u>R</u> is used to prepare documents.

13

3. Cross out the word that does NOT belong.

1. desk ~~pencil~~ bookcase
2. envelope photocopier word processor
3. typewriter receptionist pen
4. pen boss secretary
5. intercom telephone staple

4. Circle the supplies you might find in a desk drawer. (6 words)

file cabinet	(stapler)	pen	bookcase
envelope	paper	pencil	photocopier
paper clip	typist	waste paper	word processor

5. Fill in the blanks.

The R E C E P T I O N I S T is an important person in an office. She answers the T _ _ _ _ _ _ _ E, takes M _ _ _ _ _ _ S for the B _ _ S and greets visitors. Sometimes she also sorts the mail.

6. Draw a line between the noun and the corresponding activity.

NOUN	ACTIVITY
telephone	file
stapler	throw away
file cabinet	speak
word processor	call
wastepaper basket	mail
intercom	type
envelope	attach

7. Write the words for the objects below.

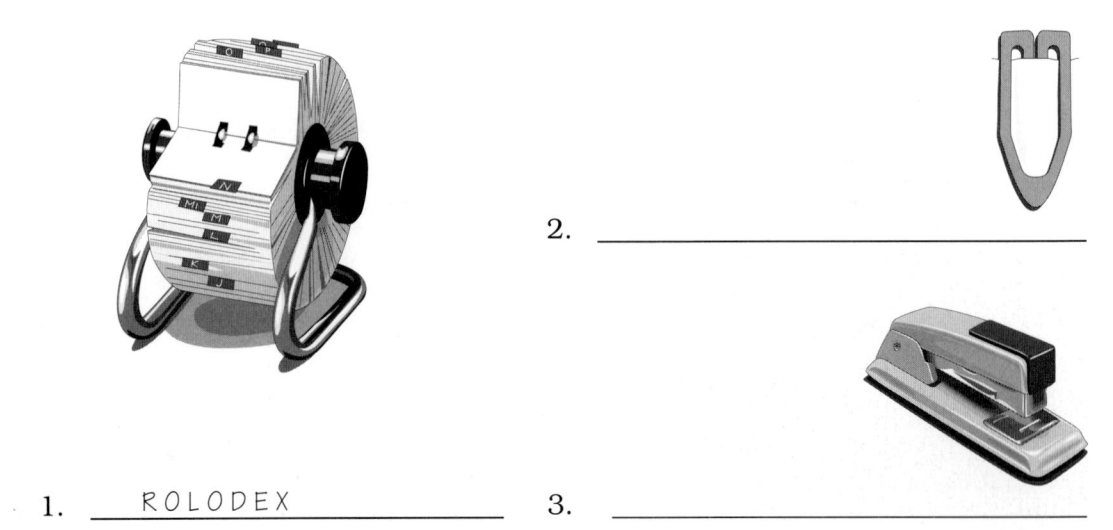

1. ROLODEX
2. _____
3. _____

14

Reading Practice

1. Which underlined word is incorrect? Circle the letter.

> **Grammar to Know:**
> conditional sentences   conjunctions
> subject-verb agreement   prepositions

1. The secretary put a paper clip <u>of</u> the loose papers and <u>returned</u> them <u>to</u>
                                                 Ⓐ   B   C
   their file in the file cabinet.

2. <u>My</u> secretary <u>use</u> a word processor rather <u>than</u> a typewriter.
     A   B   C

3. I <u>has</u> a <u>10 o'clock</u> appointment <u>with</u> my boss.
      A   B   C

4. When the receptionist <u>goes</u> <u>to</u> lunch, you should <u>answered</u> the phone.
                                  A B   C

5. Please <u>put</u> the envelope <u>at</u> <u>my</u> in-box.
          A   B C

6. The secretary <u>sat</u> at his desk <u>still</u> took the letter <u>in</u> shorthand.
                 A   B   C

7. The manager <u>order</u> some supplies: pens, a <u>stapler</u> <u>and</u> paper clips.
            A   B C

8. The number <u>was</u> among my messages, <u>which</u> were thrown <u>on</u> the
               A   B   C
   wastepaper basket.

9. If the new computer <u>and</u> photocopier <u>arrive</u> on Tuesday, we can <u>started</u>
                           A   B   C
   our project.

10. Operator, <u>will</u> you <u>connects</u> me <u>with</u> department seven?
                 A   B   C

Telephone Expressions

1. This man is on the phone.

2. The line is busy.
   The number is engaged.

3. Hang up and call back later.

2. Read the following conversation and answer the questions.

> Boss: Do you have the letter we received yesterday from the Smith Company?
> Secretary: Yes, I filed it already. Do you want to see it?
> Boss: Yes, I want to reread it before I reply.
> Secretary: Here it is. Let me photocopy it for you.

1. Who is the letter from?
   (A) The boss
   (B) The Smith Company
   (C) The secretary

2. The boss wants to see the letter before
   (A) he replies to it
   (B) it is thrown away
   (C) the secretary mails it

3. Where did the secretary put the letter?
   (A) In the in-box
   (B) In a file folder
   (C) In the mail

4. What will the secretary do with the letter?
   (A) Mail it
   (B) Fold it
   (C) Photocopy it

3. Read the following paragraph and answer the questions.

> Twenty years ago, the photocopy machine was a convenience. Today, it's a necessity for the efficient office. Photocopies of documents are exact reproductions of the original documents. They can be made quickly and cheaply.

1. When were photocopiers merely a convenience?
   (A) 15 years ago
   (B) 20 years ago
   (C) 25 years ago

2. Today the photocopy machine is an office
   (A) luxury
   (B) necessity
   (C) benefit

3. What are photocopies?
   (A) Souvenir snapshots
   (B) Carbon papers
   (C) Exact reproductions

4. How can photocopies be made?
   (A) Slowly but surely
   (B) Quickly and cheaply
   (C) Expensively and poorly

PHOTOCOPY EXPRESSIONS

1. Make 4 copies for me.

2. Copy this back-to-back. = Use both sides of the paper.

5 TYPES OF BUSINESSES

WORDS TO KNOW

art gallery	clothes store	grocery store	record store
barbershop	department store	hair salon	restaurant
beauty parlor	dress store	jewelry store	shoe store
bicycle shop	drug store	luggage store	shopping mall
cafe	fast food place	office supply store	sporting goods store
candy store	furniture store	pharmacy	toy store

WORD PRACTICE

1. Cross out the word that does NOT belong.

BUSINESS | RELATED PRODUCT OR SERVICE

1. restaurant: menu waiter ~~football~~
2. office supply store: staples pens bananas
3. jewelry store: shoes bracelets rings
4. clothes store: pants lumber dresses
5. pharmacy: aspirin drugs motor oil
6. barbershop: scissors shave boats
7. art gallery: cushions frames paintings
8. furniture store: beds lamps stationery
9. grocery store: computers fruit produce
10. sporting goods store: baseball golf club rubber band

2. Who works at these places? Circle the correct profession.

WORK PLACE | PROFESSION

1. restaurant: (chef) diner
2. jewelry store: jeweler thief
3. hair salon: hair stylist bartender
4. grocery store: gardener grocer
5. pharmacy: farmer pharmacist

3. Circle the correct word.

1. I need a new pair of shoes.
   I should go to the ((shoe store) / grocery store).

2. I need a new suitcase.
   I should go to the (clothes store / luggage store).

3. I need a new hat.
   I should go to the (hair salon / department store).

4. I need some medicine.
   I should go to the (drug store / record store).

5. I want a new record and a compact disc.
   I should go to the (record store / office supply store).

4. Look at the map of the shopping mall. Answer the questions below.

	Restaurant	Shoe Store	Toy Store	Furniture Store	Dress Shop
Department Store					
	Candy Store	Hair Salon	Drug Store	Bike Shop	Art Gallery

1. Can I buy some shoes at the mall? __YES, YOU CAN.__
   Where? __AT THE SHOE STORE. BETWEEN THE RESTAURANT AND THE TOY STORE.__

2. Can I buy a toy for my niece? _____
   Where? _____

3. Can I get my hair cut? _____
   Where? _____

4. Can I buy a new bike? _____
   Where? _____

5. Can I look at some bedroom furniture? _____
   Where? _____

5. Draw a line between the business and a product available at the business.

BUSINESS	PRODUCT
1. toy store	sandals
2. record store	prescription medicine
3. candy store	overnight bags
4. bicycle shop	dolls
5. pharmacy	compact discs
6. shoe store	racing bikes
7. luggage store	chocolate bars

READING PRACTICE

1. Which underlined word is incorrect? Circle the letter.

> **GRAMMAR TO KNOW:**
> articles   prepositions
> subject-verb agreement   gerunds

1. The art gallery is having <u>an</u> <u>open</u> <u>on</u> Friday night.
                                    A   (B) C

2. Today I must <u>go</u> <u>at</u> the pharmacy, the hair salon <u>and</u> the grocery store.
                  A B   C

3. I prefer the small cafe <u>on</u> Main Street because <u>the</u> restaurant <u>are</u> noisy.
                             A   B   C

4. My son just <u>got</u> a job <u>of</u> the record store <u>in</u> the shopping mall.
                 A   B   C

5. Barbara always enjoys <u>to shop</u> <u>in</u> small dress stores <u>rather</u> than large
                      A   B   C
   department stores.

6. <u>The</u> new luggage store <u>is doing</u> a lot of <u>the</u> business already.
     A   B   C

7. Candy stores, fast food places <u>and</u> bicycle shops <u>are</u> a few places where
                              A   B
   young teenagers <u>goes</u>.
                     C

8. The barbershop put the beauty parlor out <u>of</u> business because it <u>gave</u>
                                        A   B
   <u>the</u> less expensive haircuts.
    C

9. <u>The</u> beautiful windows <u>of</u> the new jewelry store <u>attracts</u> a lot of customers.
     A   B   C

10. Surprised that <u>the</u> office supply store didn't <u>have</u> office chairs, the man
                         A   B
    went <u>of</u> the furniture store.
          C

19

2. Read the following passage and answer the questions.

> The shopping mall has four floors of shops. There are small specialty shops selling imported shoes and clothes, and two large department stores which sell everything. On the first level are ten fast food places selling food from all parts of the world.

1. What is the passage about?
   (A) Import taxes
   (B) Shoe styles
   (C) A shopping mall

2. How many floors are there?
   (A) One
   (B) Two
   (C) Four

3. What's on the first level?
   (A) Fast food places
   (B) Imported shoes
   (C) Department stores

4. Where is the food from?
   (A) The neighborhood
   (B) The suburbs
   (C) All over the world

3. Read the following conversation and answer the questions:

> Bob: Can you tell me where the shoe store is?
> Mary: Yes, it's on Main Street between the hair salon and the record store.
> Bob: Is it across from the jewelry store?
> Mary: No, it's across from the pharmacy.

1. Where is the shoe store?
   (A) By the jewelry store
   (B) Across from the record store
   (C) Next to the hair salon

2. Which is NOT on Main Street?
   (A) Hair salon
   (B) Shoe store
   (C) Police station

3. Where is the record store?
   (A) Next to the shoe store
   (B) Across from the jewelry store
   (C) Next to the pharmacy

4. Where is the pharmacy?
   (A) Across from the shoe store
   (B) Next to the jewelry store
   (C) Next to the hair salon

6 RESTAURANTS

WORDS TO KNOW

ashtray	cup	menu	smoking section
bar	dessert	napkin	snack
bartender	diner	order	soft drink
bill	dinner	plate	spoon
breakfast	fork	reservation	supper
cafe	glass	restaurant	tablecloth
captain	knife	saucer	tip
check	lunch	service	waiter
coffee	meal	silverware	waitress

WORD PRACTICE

1. Complete the following sentences.

1. It is good to eat B R E A K F A S T in the morning.

2. At busy restaurants a R _ _ _ _ V _ _ _ _ _ is necessary.

3. A B _ _ T _ _ _ _ _ serves drinks at the bar.

4. The L _ _ _ _ hour falls between 11:30 and 1:00 p.m.

5. A 15% S _ _ _ _ _ E charge is added to the bill.

2. Write which meal or snack is usually eaten 1st, 2nd, 3rd, and 4th.

CHOICES: dinner, afternoon snack, breakfast, lunch

1st meal _____

2nd meal _____

3rd meal _____

4th meal _____

21

3. Write the appropriate adjective.

CHOICES: dirty, slow, cold, high, smoky

1. This coffee is _____COLD_____.
2. This bill is too _____.
3. The service is very _____.
4. The spoon is _____.
5. The smoking section is very _____.

4. Complete the following items you put on a table.

1. C U P
2. N _ _ _ _ _
3. G _ _ _ S _ _
4. S _ _ _ _
5. P _ _ _ E
6. F _ _ _
7. K N _ _ _
8. S A _ _ _ _
9. T _ _ _ _ C L _ _ _

5. Write the correct word in the blank for each of the definitions below.

| ashtray | soft drink | smoking section | tip |
| check | snack | waitress | silverware |

1. A container for cigarette ashes   _____ASHTRAY_____
2. A sweet carbonated drink   _____
3. A woman who serves food   _____
4. An area for people who smoke   _____
5. Food eaten between meals   _____
6. A bill for restaurant meals   _____
7. Extra money for the waiter or waitress   _____
8. Knives, forks, spoons, etc.   _____

6. Circle the correct adverb of frequency.

1. A waiter ((always) / never) takes an order.

2. Restaurants (never / always) have tables.

3. A reservation is (always / sometimes) necessary for dinner.

4. Customers should (sometimes / never) leave without tipping.

5. Napkins are (sometimes / always) made of paper.

READING PRACTICE

1. Which underlined word is incorrect? Circle the letter.

> **GRAMMAR TO KNOW:**
> conjunctions   modal auxiliaries
> pronouns   subject-verb agreement

1. I <u>will</u> like <u>to order</u> a cup of coffee <u>with</u> my breakfast, please.
   (A)   B   C

2. Bill <u>looked</u> at <u>the</u> menu a long time <u>while</u> then ordered only coffee.
     A   B   C

3. <u>Puts</u> your cigarette out, please. This <u>is</u> not <u>the</u> smoking section.
    A   B   C

4. The waitress, <u>hoping</u> <u>her</u> would get a big tip, <u>put</u> the check on the table.
                  A   B   C

5. This restaurant is <u>busy</u> and <u>would</u> only <u>seat</u> parties with a reservation.
                     A   B   C

6. <u>Let's</u> go <u>to</u> a late-night snack <u>at</u> the diner.
    A   B   C

7. Waiter, there <u>is</u> a spot <u>on</u> my spoon, <u>but</u> this tablecloth is filthy!
             A   B   C

8. You <u>should</u> always <u>used</u> the small fork when <u>eating</u> a salad.
       A   B   C

9. The bartender <u>enjoys</u> <u>talking</u> to people who are on <u>his</u> lunch break.
               A   B   C

10. This restaurant <u>are</u> famous <u>for</u> its selection <u>of</u> rich desserts.
              A   B   C

2. Read the following conversation and answer the questions.

> Waiter: I hope you have enjoyed your meal.
> Customer: It was very good.
> Waiter: Would you like to see the dessert menu?
> Customer: No, thank you. But I would like a cup of coffee.
> Waiter: Fine. Anything else?
> Customer: No... could you bring my check with the coffee?
> Waiter: Certainly.

1. The customer has just finished his
   (A) coffee
   (B) dessert
   (C) meal

2. What does the waiter offer the customer?
   (A) A cup of coffee
   (B) The dessert menu
   (C) His check

3. When does the customer want his check?
   (A) After his coffee
   (B) Before his coffee
   (C) With his coffee

4. After the customer finishes his coffee, he will
   (A) pay the check
   (B) order a meal
   (C) have dessert

3. Read the following and answer the questions.

> When diners in a restaurant finish their meal, they pay their check and leave. The waiter quickly prepares the table for other customers. He first takes away the dirty dishes and napkins. He then changes the tablecloth. He cleans out the ashtray and places it in the center of the table with the salt and pepper. Finally, he places clean plates, glasses, and silverware on the table.

1. How does the waiter work?
   (A) Slowly
   (B) Quickly
   (C) Carelessly

2. Why does he remove the dishes?
   (A) They are ready.
   (B) They are dirty.
   (C) They are new.

3. What does the waiter change?
   (A) The ashtray
   (B) The chairs
   (C) The tablecloth

4. Where does the waiter put the ashtray?
   (A) On another table
   (B) Next to the salt and pepper
   (C) On top of the napkin

7 OFFICE TERMS

WORDS TO KNOW

answering machine	drawer	floppy disk	photocopy
boss	electric typewriter	folder	printer
clerical work	envelope	letter	secretary
client	fax (facsimile)	mail	telephone
computer	fax machine	manager	typist
courier	file	memorandum	typo
diskette	file cabinet	mistake	word processor

WORD PRACTICE

1. Complete the following sentences.

1. A good T Y P I S T usually types over 90 words a minute.
2. A typist often works in an O _ _ _ _ _ .
3. Important business papers are filed by the clerical worker in a
   F _ _ _   C _ _ _ _ E T .
4. Put the letter in a large E _ _ _ _ _ _ _ and stamp it.
5. If you make a M I _ _ _ _ E , please correct it.
6. Each worker sits at his own D _ _ _ .
7. The C L _ _ _ _ _ _ workers must file all the correspondence.
8. The office M _ _ _ _ _ R sent a memo to all the typists.

2. Draw a line between words that are associated with one another.

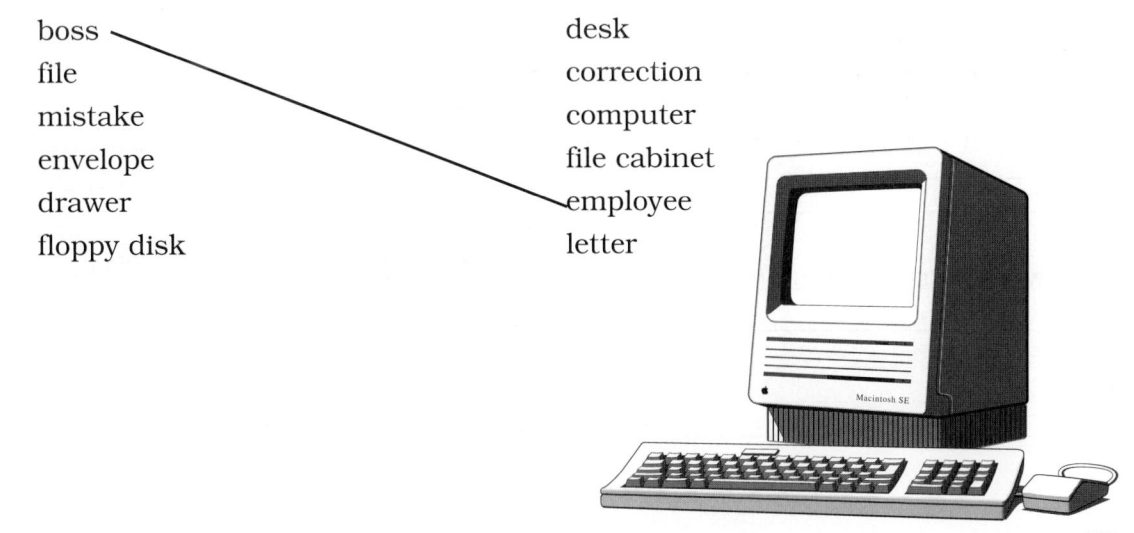

boss — employee
file
mistake
envelope
drawer
floppy disk

desk
correction
computer
file cabinet
letter

25

3. Write the word under the appropriate label.

	MACHINES	PEOPLE
fax machine	FAX MACHINE	
boss		BOSS
answering machine		
secretary		
computer		
typist		
employee		
client		
telephone		
word processor		
photocopier		

4. Draw a line between the word and its abbreviation.

WORD	ABBREVIATION
typographical mistake	memo
facsimile	phone
photocopy	typo
memorandum	fax
telephone	copy

(line drawn from "typographical mistake" to "typo")

5. Write these words under the appropriate label.

memorandum   electric typewriter   word processor   by hand (2)
mail   fax (2)   letter   courier

TYPES OF BUSINESS CORRESPONDENCE
MEMORANDUM
_____
_____

WAYS TO PREPARE CORRESPONDENCE
_____
_____
_____

WAYS TO SEND CORRESPONDENCE
_____
_____
_____
_____

26

6. Cross out the word that does NOT belong.

1. envelope   ~~floppy disk~~   letter   paper
2. pencil   typewriter   computer   photocopier
3. boss   photocopy   typist   secretary
4. fax   mail   telephone   drawer
5. desk   office   mistakes   filing cabinet

READING PRACTICE

1. Which underlined word is incorrect? Circle the letter.

> **GRAMMAR TO KNOW:**
> infinitives   prepositions
> subject-verb agreement   verb tense

1. Please <u>stores</u> all <u>of</u> your files <u>on</u> this floppy disk.
   (A)   B   C

2. When the paper <u>becomes</u> jammed <u>in</u> the printer, the secretary went <u>to tell</u>
                    A   B   C
   the boss.

3. This <u>is</u> our new employee. Will you <u>show</u> him how <u>sending</u> a fax?
        A   B   C

4. If the typist <u>make</u> a mistake <u>on</u> the word processor, he can <u>fix</u> it easily.
                 A   B   C

5. There <u>is</u> a lot of clerical work, <u>including</u> filing, involved <u>of</u> your job.
         A   B   C

6. A secretary <u>answered</u> the <u>phone</u>, types letters, <u>and</u> sends memoranda.
               A   B   C

7. <u>Was</u> there a letter <u>of</u> Miss Collins <u>in</u> today's mail?
   A   B   C

8. The file <u>to be</u> in a folder <u>on</u> top <u>of</u> the filing cabinet.
            A   B   C

9. <u>Every</u> morning, Mr. Suarez <u>putting</u> his umbrella <u>in</u> the third drawer of his
   A   B   C
   desk.

10. The envelope was <u>too</u> small <u>holding</u> the manager's <u>report</u>.
                    A   B   C

27

2. Read the following paragraph and answer the questions.

> Miss Cordell is a typist. She works in a small office. She types letters and mails them. Before she sends a letter, she makes a photocopy and puts the copy in the files.

1. What is Miss Cordell's profession?
   - (A) Mail carrier
   - (B) Typist
   - (C) Office manager

2. Where does Miss Cordell work?
   - (A) A store
   - (B) An office
   - (C) A school

3. Miss Cordell makes a photocopy after she
   - (A) types a letter
   - (B) mails a letter
   - (C) files a letter

4. What does Miss Cordell put in the files?
   - (A) A copy of a letter
   - (B) A pencil
   - (C) The mail

3. Read the following conversation and answer the questions.

> Boss: Did you finish typing the fax?
> Secretary: Yes. Do you want it to be sent today?
> Boss: As soon as possible. Can you do it now?
> Secretary: I'm just filing letters, so I'll do the filing later, and I'll send out the fax right away.
> Boss: Great. Our client will have it when he gets back from lunch.

1. When should the fax be sent?
   - (A) This morning
   - (B) Immediately
   - (C) After lunch

2. What is the typist doing now?
   - (A) Sending the fax
   - (B) Typing the fax
   - (C) Filing letters

3. Who is sending the fax?
   - (A) The client
   - (B) A restaurant chef
   - (C) The secretary

4. Who will receive the fax?
   - (A) A client
   - (B) A chef
   - (C) The mailman

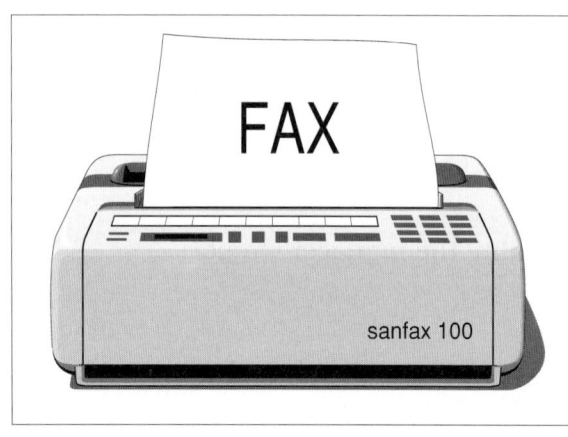

FAX EXPRESSIONS

1. I received a fax.
2. I sent a fax.
3. I faxed a letter to him.
4. Fax me your proposal.
5. She'll fax it to me later.
6. What is your fax number?

8 CONSTRUCTION

WORDS TO KNOW

bathtub	foreman	paint	screwdriver
board	fuse	painter	shower
burned out	glue	pipe	shower head
carpenter	hammer	plaster	sink
connect	handyman	plug	switch
contractor	homeowner	plumber	tool
current	inch	plunger	toolbox
drain	lamp	power	turn on/off
drill	leak	ruler	washer
drip	measure	running water	wire
electrician	metal	sand	wood
faucet	meter	sandpaper	woodwork
file	nail	saw	work bench
fixture	outlets	screw	wrench

WORD PRACTICE

1. Draw a line between associated words.

VERB	NOUN
to hammer	sand paper
to measure	nail
to cut	power
to drain	screwdriver
to screw	ruler
to sand	saw
to turn on	sink

2. Fill in the blanks.

A Carpenter

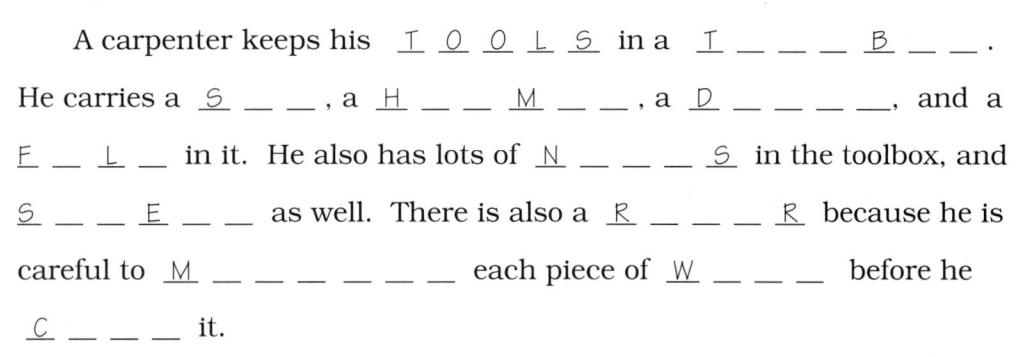

A carpenter keeps his T O O L S in a T _ _ _ B _ _ . He carries a S _ _ , a H _ _ M _ _ , a D _ _ _ _ _, and a F _ L _ in it. He also has lots of N _ _ _ S in the toolbox, and S _ _ E _ _ as well. There is also a R _ _ _ R because he is careful to M _ _ _ _ _ _ each piece of W _ _ _ before he C _ _ _ it.

29

3. Complete these sentences by adding *-ing* to the words in parentheses.

> **NOTE THESE DIFFERENCES:**
> drip   dripping
> plug   plugging

1. The carpenter is (saw) __SAWING__ a piece of wood into two pieces.
2. The handyman is (hammer) _____ a nail into the wall.
3. The foreman is (drill) _____ a hole for a screw.
4. The painter is (sand) _____ the wood to make it smooth.
5. The plumber is (drain) _____ the water from the sink.
6. The water is (leak) _____ from the faucet.
7. The shower head is (drip) _____ water.
8. The electrician is (plug) _____ the lamp into the outlet.
9. The contractor is (turn on) _____ the power to the house.
10. The homeowner is (look for) _____ a burned-out fuse.

4. Cross out the word that does NOT belong.

1. nail / ~~ruler~~ / screw
2. leak / saw / board
3. fuse / sandpaper / file
4. board / screwdriver / wood
5. switch / turn on / sink
6. measure / light / lamp
7. turn off / power / work bench
8. current / meter / window
9. wire / faucet / running water
10. bathtub / saw / shower

5. Draw a line to create a new compound noun. Write the new compound noun.

NOUN	+	NOUN	COMPOUND NOUN
bath		driver	BATHTUB
sand		bench	_____
tool		tub	_____
work		paper	_____
screw		box	_____

30

6. Fill in the blanks.

A Plumber

Sometime water does not drain from a sink. If a S̲ __ __ __ doesn't drain, something may be plugging the D̲ R̲ __ __ __. If the drain is stopped up, the P̲ __ __ M̲ __ __ __ may use a tool called a P̲ __ __ N̲ __ __ __ to clear the P̲ __ __ __ S̲.

READING PRACTICE

1. Which underlined word is incorrect? Circle the letter.

> **GRAMMAR TO KNOW:**
> conditional sentences   gerunds
> prepositions   verb tense

1. Please <u>use</u> sandpaper <u>in</u> the woodwork to make <u>it</u> smooth.
        A   Ⓑ   C
2. The plywood <u>that</u> the carpenter <u>use</u> was not thick enough <u>for</u> the wall.
            A   B   C
3. The electrician <u>connecting</u> the wall fixtures safely <u>to</u> the <u>nearest</u> outlets.
               A   B   C
4. There <u>is</u> a problem <u>for</u> the electrical outlets <u>in</u> this house.
        A   B   C
5. If <u>the</u> toilet <u>would</u> not <u>flush</u>, the plumber uses the plunger.
     A   B   C
6. Katherine opened the plug to <u>letting</u> the water <u>drain</u> out <u>of</u> the sink.
               A   B   C
7. The plumber will <u>came</u> tomorrow <u>to fix</u> the <u>leaking</u> pipe in the kitchen.
          A   B   C
8. <u>Always</u> <u>turned</u> off all the lights before you <u>leave</u> the house.
     A   B   C
9. The electrician came <u>to</u> our house and <u>fix</u> <u>the</u> wires yesterday.
             A   B C
10. Today the carpenters <u>will</u> install the glass <u>at</u> all <u>of</u> the windows.
             A   B   C

> A hardhat must be worn at all construction sites.
>
> Construction workers are often called "hardhats."

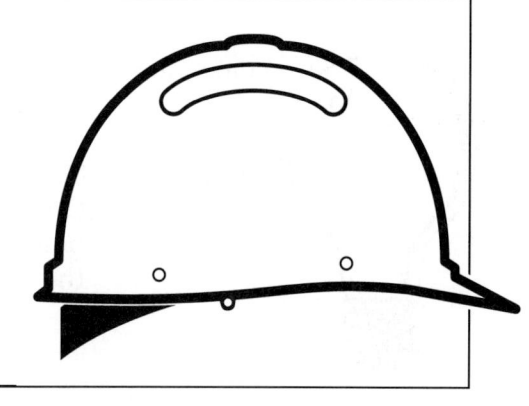

2. Read the following paragraph and answer the questions.

> Some electrical problems can be easily fixed. When a light bulb burns out, you can easily replace it. When a fuse burns out, you can lose all electric power to a house. You can easily replace the fuse yourself. You can do small wiring jobs at home. Large wiring jobs should be done by an electrician.

1. What is an example of an easy electrical problem?
   - (A) An electrical fire
   - (B) A burned-out bulb
   - (C) Complicated wiring

2. What can return electric power to a house?
   - (A) A telephone call
   - (B) A new fuse
   - (C) Solar power

3. Who should be called for large wiring jobs?
   - (A) A plumber
   - (B) A carpenter
   - (C) An electrician

4. This passage discusses electricity
   - (A) on the job
   - (B) at home
   - (C) at night

3. Read the following conversation and answer the questions.

> Plumber: Hello. ABC Plumbing.
> Customer: Hello. I need a plumber.
> Plumber: What's the problem?
> Customer: A leaky faucet. It's been dripping for a week. It won't stop dripping.
> Plumber: OK. We'll be there tomorrow morning.

1. Where does this conversation take place?
   - (A) On the telephone
   - (B) In a plumbing supply shop
   - (C) At the front door

2. What is the name of the plumbing company?
   - (A) OK Plumbing
   - (B) Hello Plumbing
   - (C) ABC Plumbing

3. What is the problem?
   - (A) No hot water
   - (B) A leaky faucet
   - (C) A dripping shower

4. When will the plumber come?
   - (A) Right away
   - (B) Next week
   - (C) Tomorrow

Question: How many English teachers does it take to screw in a lightbulb?

Answer: Three. One to hold the bulb. One to hold the ladder. And one to read the directions.

9 ENTERTAINING

WORDS TO KNOW

actor/actress	classical	music	program
aisle	comedian	musical	rock
attend	comedy	musician	row
audience	concert	opera	seat
balcony	conductor	orchestra	singer
box	director	performer	stage
cast	drama	play	star
chorus	film	playhouse	symphony
circus	intermission	popcorn	theater
cinema	movie	popular	ticket

WORD PRACTICE

1. Write the noun for the person which matches the verb.

VERB	NOUN
1. conduct	<u>CONDUCTOR</u>
2. direct	_____
3. act	_____ or _____
4. perform	_____
5. sing	_____

2. Cross out the word in each of the following groups that does NOT belong.

1. music:	opera	symphony	~~seat~~	
2. theater:	play	television	movie	
3. cast:	actor	laughter	actress	
4. seat:	balcony	music	row	
5. perform:	sit	act	sing	

3. Circle the words below for types of entertainment. (7 words)

(concert)	ticket	seat	movie
box	opera	musical	row
symphony	play	intermission	comedy

33

4. Fill in the blanks.

Music

    There are many kinds of musical entertainment. One kind is C _ _ _ _ _ _ L ; two examples of this kind of music are the S _ _ _ _ _ _ Y and the O _ _ _ A . Another kind of musical entertainment is the M _ _ _ _ _ L play, which is more popular than opera. Most popular of all is R _ _ K.

5. Draw a line between words that are the same or similar in meaning.

1. opera   concert
2. film   conductor
3. symphony   play
4. drama   actress
5. director   musical
6. star   movie

(lines drawn: opera — musical; drama — concert)

6. Write the word under the appropriate category.

	PERSON	ACTION	LOCATION
actor	ACTOR		
attend		ATTEND	
audience			
balcony			BALCONY
box			
cast			
chorus			
cinema			
conduct			
direct			
musician			
perform			

7. Complete the following questions.

    CHOICES: playhouse, cast, row, chorus

1. What is an INTERMISSION ?
   A break between acts in a play

2. What is a _____ ?
   The entire company of performers in a performance

3. What is a _____ ?
   A group of singers and dancers who do not have major parts

4. What is a _____ ?
   A section of seats running between aisles

5. What is a _____ ?
   A small theater

Reading Practice

1. Which underlined word is incorrect? Circle the letter.

> **GRAMMAR TO KNOW:**
> conjunctions   gerunds
> infinitives   prepositions

1. We <u>were</u> lucky to <u>getting</u> box seats <u>for</u> Friday's concert.
      A   (B)   C

2. Would you like to go <u>see</u> a movie at the cinema <u>nor</u> a play <u>at</u> the theater?
                      A   B   C

3. Scott's <u>parents</u> <u>preferring</u> classical music <u>to</u> rock music.
       A   B   C

4. <u>My</u> favorite actress <u>is</u> <u>at</u> the chorus in this old movie.
    A   B C

5. The star <u>to perform</u> currently in this opera <u>is</u> <u>a</u> former dramatic actor.
         A   B C

6. <u>The</u> conductor <u>in</u> the city's symphony orchestra is well-<u>known</u>.
    A   B   C

7. Some musicians <u>performs</u> <u>to please</u> themselves <u>rather than</u> please their audience.
                   A   B   C

8. Most people <u>buy</u> popcorn <u>eating</u> during the intermission <u>of</u> the film.
            A   B   C

9. If you'd like <u>using</u> my tickets <u>for</u> the musical comedy, you <u>may</u>.
           A   B   C

10. We <u>have</u> fourth-row tickets <u>of</u> <u>the</u> circus tonight.
       A   B C

MUSICAL EXPRESSIONS

<u>Positive Expressions</u>
She sings like a bird.
She has a song in her heart.
She has a golden throat.

<u>Negative Expressions</u>
She has a voice like a bullfrog.
She can't carry a tune.
She couldn't carry a tune in a bucket.
She's tone deaf.
Her voice would shatter glass.

2. Read the following paragraph and answer the questions.

> Many people enjoy seeing movies in a theater. They pay for their tickets at the box office. Then they might buy some popcorn to eat during the movie. Before the movie begins, there are often advertisements for coming attractions.

1. Where do many people like to see movies?
   - (A) At home
   - (B) In a theater
   - (C) On TV

2. Where do people get tickets for a movie?
   - (A) At the box office
   - (B) At their seats
   - (C) From their friends

3. People at a movie sometimes eat
   - (A) hot dogs
   - (B) corn on the cob
   - (C) popcorn

4. What are coming attractions?
   - (A) Movies to be seen soon
   - (B) Unwanted guests
   - (C) Magnets

3. Read the following conversation and answer the questions.

> John: Let's see a Broadway play while we're visiting New York next month.
> Mary: Theater tickets are too expensive.
> John: We can get cheap seats—in the balcony, for instance.
> Mary: Okay, but we'd better buy our tickets soon. Broadway shows are often sold out weeks in advance.

1. When are they visiting New York?
   - (A) Next week
   - (B) Next month
   - (C) Next year

2. What does John want to do in New York?
   - (A) Go to a theater
   - (B) See the Statue of Liberty
   - (C) Attend a game

3. Where are the cheap seats in a theater?
   - (A) On Broadway
   - (B) In the balcony
   - (C) In the orchestra

4. Mary says that tickets for Broadway shows are often
   - (A) easy to get
   - (B) cheap
   - (C) sold out

10 TEACHING

WORDS TO KNOW

absent	engineering	learn	records
arithmetic	English	lecture	review
assignment	enrollment	liberal arts	science
attendance	examination	literature	score
blackboard	fail	major	seminar
bulletin board	foreign language	mathematics	senior
chalk	freshman	music	sophomore
check	grade	notes	student
class	grammar	pass	study
correct	history	present	teacher
course	homework	professor	test
economics	junior	pupil	text
elementary	laboratory	quiz	workbook

WORD PRACTICE

1. Draw a line between words with similar meanings.

1. pupil
2. mathematics
3. professor
4. book
5. learn
6. subject
6. correct
7. test

course
examination
student
study
text
check
arithmetic
teacher

2. Write the Progressive Form of the verbs below by adding *-ing*.

1. teach   TEACHING
2. study   _____
3. learn   _____
4. major   _____
5. attend   _____
6. review   _____
7. check   _____
8. test   _____

3. Use these words to complete the sentences.

CHOICES: take, keep, learn, fail, solve

1. Secretaries _____KEEP_____ school records.
2. Math students _____ problems.
3. It is difficult to _____ some languages.
4. Teachers must _____ attendance.
5. Students _____ if they don't study.

4. Write the plural nouns in their singular forms.

PLURAL NOUN	SINGULAR NOUN
1. studies	STUDY
2. laboratories	
3. histories	
4. economies	
5. difficulties	

5. Write the noun form.

VERB	NOUN
1. attend	ATTENDANCE
2. enroll	
3. correct	
4. examine	

6. Complete the sentences.

1. I am in my first year of college.
   I am a F _ _ _ _ _ _ _ _.
2. I am in my second year of college.
   I am a S _ _ _ _ _ _ _ _.
3. I am in my third year of college.
   I am a J _ _ _ _ _ _.
4. I am in my fourth year of college.
   I am a S _ _ _ _ _.

7. Complete the sentences.

1. The <u>T E A C H E R</u> stands in front of the class.
2. The <u>S T _ _ _ _ _ _</u> are at their desks.
3. Grades are posted on the <u>B _ _ L _ _ _ _</u> <u>B _ _ _ _</u>.
4. Our homework <u>A S _ _ _ _ _ _ _ _</u> was very difficult.
5. You must take this <u>C _ _ _ S _</u> in order to graduate.
6. The first six years of school are usually known as

   <u>E _ _ _ _ _ _ _ _ _</u> school.
7. A <u>S _ M _ _ _ _</u> is a lecture or discussion on one subject.

READING PRACTICE

1. Which underlined word is incorrect? Circle the letter.

> **GRAMMAR TO KNOW:**
> conjunctions   infinitives
> prepositions   verb tense

1. <u>During</u> Anthony's freshman year, he <u>enrolled</u> <u>of</u> two English courses.
     A   B   Ⓒ

2. Attendance <u>is</u> necessary <u>passing</u> <u>physical</u> education.
                 A   B   C

3. The teacher <u>told</u> the pupils to <u>passed</u> their books <u>to</u> the front of the room.
            A   B   C

4. Tonight Jack <u>should</u> do homework <u>for</u> history, economics, <u>also</u> literature.
                 A   B   C

5. Tomorrow there <u>will</u> be a mathematics quiz so <u>be</u> sure <u>studying</u> the text.
                 A   B   C

6. All of the students <u>in</u> biology class must <u>brought</u> their workbooks <u>to</u>
                         A   B   C
   the laboratory.

7. <u>During</u> my junior year, I <u>got</u> good grades <u>at</u> most of my courses.
     A   B   C

8. The professor <u>lectured</u> <u>for</u> two hours <u>still</u> the students took notes.
                  A   B   C

9. If your <u>attendance</u> does not <u>improve</u>, you will <u>failed</u> this class.
            A   B   C

10. Please <u>exchange</u> your tests <u>so</u> you can <u>corrected</u> each other's work.
              A   B   C

2. Read the following passage and answer the questions.

> Everyday the teacher takes attendance by marking which students are present and which are absent. This information is kept in a book along with the students' test scores. Students' attendance records may affect their final grade.

1. Where is attendance information kept?
   (A) In a textbook
   (B) On the bulletin board
   (C) In a record book

2. Who takes attendance?
   (A) The students
   (B) The teacher
   (C) The secretary

3. What does attendance mean?
   (A) Presence
   (B) Grades
   (C) Test scores

4. Students' attendance records can affect
   (A) their test scores
   (B) their note taking
   (C) their final grades

3. Read the following conversation and answer the questions.

> Student: Are we going to check the homework today?
> Teacher: Yes. We'll go over it after a short quiz.
> Student: What subject is our quiz on?
> Teacher: Literature. I hope everybody read his homework assignment last night.
> Student: I did my math instead.

1. When are they going to check the homework?
   (A) Before a quiz
   (B) After a quiz
   (C) Tomorrow

2. Which of his homework did the student NOT do?
   (A) Literature
   (B) Reading
   (C) Math

3. The teacher hopes that everybody
   (A) finished his math
   (B) read his homework assignment
   (C) checked his homework

4. What did the student do last night?
   (A) Did his math homework
   (B) Went to a movie
   (C) Played football

SCHOOL EXPRESSION

An apple for the teacher.

11 MEDICINE

WORDS TO KNOW

ache	doctor	infection	physician
ambulance	drill	injection	pill
aspirin	drug store	injury	prescription
bandage	emergency	medication	sick
bone	fever	medicine	sore
broken	headache	nurse	technician
clinic	heal	operation	temperature
cold	hospital	pain	tooth / teeth
cure	hurt	patient	toothache
dentist	ill	pharmacist	treatment
disease	illness	pharmacy	x-ray

WORD PRACTICE

1. Draw a line between words with similar meanings.

fever — temperature
hurt — ill
medication — disease
physician — doctor
sick — medicine
illness — ache

2. Complete the sentences.

1. A T E C H N I C I A N works in a laboratory.
2. A tooth problem is treated by a D _ _ _ _ _ T.
3. A doctor takes care of P _ _ _ _ _ _ _.
4. A B _ _ _ _ _ bone will heal.
5. A pharmacist fills a P _ _ _ _ _ _ _ _ _ _ _.

3. Write the noun forms of the verbs below.

VERB	NOUN	VERB	NOUN
1. prescribe	PRESCRIPTION	4. injure	
2. medicate		5. treat	
3. operate		6. infect	

41

4. Write the words associated with doctors or dentists under the labels. Some words are used twice.

| a cold | drill | headache | toothache |
| x-ray | broken | tooth | infection |

DOCTORS

A COLD
_____
_____
_____
_____
_____
_____

DENTISTS

DRILL
_____
_____
_____
_____
_____
_____

5. Cross out the word that does NOT belong.

1. sick — ~~bandage~~ — ill
2. doctor — physician — operation
3. a cold — medication — prescription
4. ambulance — dentist — toothache
5. broken — treat — cure
6. aspirin — medicine — x ray
7. clinic — technician — hospital

6. Fill in the blanks.

In the Hospital

When a P _ _ _ _ _ T is in the H O _ _ _ _ _ _ _, he usually stays in bed. The N _ R _ _ brings him what he needs. She brings M _ _ _ _ A _ _ _ _ and P _ _ L S and gives I N _ _ _ _ _ _ _. If the patient needs an X _ _ _ or an O _ _ R _ _ _ _ _, she helps him prepare for it. Usually the D _ _ _ _ R will come in once a day for a short visit.

A nurse's cap can tell us where the nurse went to school. Each nursing school has its own cap.

7. Write the word under the appropriate category.

	PERSON	CONDITION	THING
prescription	_____	_____	PRESCRIPTION
ache	_____	ACHE	_____
bandage	_____	_____	_____
dentist	DENTIST	_____	_____
fever	_____	_____	_____
headache	_____	_____	_____
infection	_____	_____	_____
medicine	_____	_____	_____
nurse	_____	_____	_____
patient	_____	_____	_____
sore	_____	_____	_____
technician	_____	_____	_____
pharmacy	_____	_____	_____

READING PRACTICE

1. Which underlined word is incorrect? Circle the letter.

> **GRAMMAR TO KNOW:**
> conjunctions   infinitives
> prepositions   verb tense

1. This patient <u>is</u> very sick <u>or</u> should be <u>taken</u> to the hospital immediately.
           A   (B)   C

2. Are you <u>under</u> <u>a</u> physician's order <u>taking</u> that medication?
       A B   C

3. There <u>is</u> a cure <u>at</u> this disease, but <u>the</u> drugs are very expensive.
      A   B   C

4. The medics <u>on</u> the ambulance were able <u>saving</u> the patient's life before
           A   B
   they arrived <u>at</u> the emergency room.
            C

5. The doctor <u>removing</u> the bandages to <u>see</u> if the infection had <u>healed</u>.
           A   B   C

6. Because <u>the</u> patient was <u>in</u> pain, the nurse <u>gives</u> her medication.
          A   B   C

7. A fever <u>also</u> a headache could <u>be</u> signs of <u>a</u> more serious illness.
       A   B   C

8. The dentist drilled <u>through</u> the tooth to get <u>of</u> the source <u>of</u> the pain.
            A   B   C

9. If you <u>are staying</u> in bed <u>for</u> a few days, the soreness will <u>disappear</u>.
       A   B   C

10. <u>The</u> x-ray revealed that Sally <u>has</u> <u>a</u> broken bone.
     A   B C

2. Read the following conversation and answer the questions.

> Doctor: What seems to be the problem?
> Patient: I have a fever. My temperature is over 102 degrees.
> Doctor: You seem to have an infection on your hand.
> Patient: Yes. I cut myself yesterday with a knife.
> Doctor: Take this prescription to the drugstore. This medicine will cure the infection.

1. What is the patient's problem?
   (A) A cold
   (B) An infection
   (C) A broken bone

2. Where is the patient's infection?
   (A) On the hand
   (B) On the face
   (C) On the feet

3. How did the patient hurt himself?
   (A) With a bat
   (B) With a pencil
   (C) With a knife

4. Where will the prescription be filled?
   (A) At the drugstore
   (B) At the doctor's office
   (C) In the kitchen

3. Read the following passage and answer the questions.

> Mr. Jones had an operation yesterday. He is not in pain now, because the nurse has given him an injection. He also has taken some pills to help him relax. He can see a bandage on his stomach. Mr. Jones is glad the operation is finished.

1. Mr. Jones is probably in a
   (A) cafeteria
   (B) car
   (C) hospital

2. Where was Mr. Jones's problem?
   (A) In his stomach
   (B) On his back
   (C) In his leg

3. What helps Mr. Jones relax?
   (A) The operation
   (B) Some medication
   (C) The doctor

4. How does Mr. Jones feel about the operation?
   (A) He wants to do it again.
   (B) He is still afraid.
   (C) He is glad it is over.

MEDICAL SYMBOL

This is the international symbol of the medical profession: Two serpents entwined around a winged staff.

12 HOTEL SERVICE

WORDS TO KNOW

bellman	elevator	key	reservation
check in	elevator operator	lobby	reserve
check out	escort	lounge	room
clerk	floor	luggage	room service
desk	front desk	maid	suite
doorman	guest	make up	tip
double bed	housekeeping	register	towel

WORD PRACTICE

1. Complete the following sentences.

1. It is a good idea to R E S _ _ _ _ a room in a hotel in advance.
2. Guests R _ _ _ _ _ _ R when they C _ _ _ _ I _ .
3. Guests pay when they C _ _ _ _ _ _ _ .
4. Guests T _ _ the bellman for carrying the L U _ _ _ _ _ .

2. Draw a line between the words to make noun phrases. Write the noun phrase.

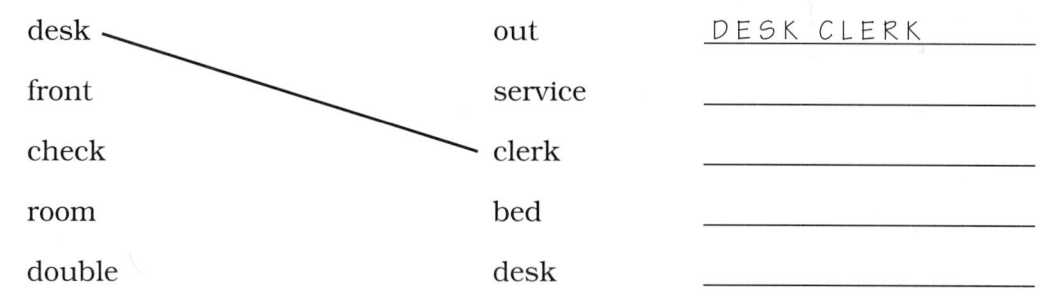

desk —————————→ clerk   DESK CLERK
front   service   _____
check   clerk   _____
room   bed   _____
double   desk   _____

(desk connects to clerk)

3. Write the words from Exercise 2 next to the correct definition.

DEFINITION	WORD
1. The place to register at a hotel	FRONT DESK
2. The person who registers hotel guests	_____
3. Pay and leave a hotel	_____
4. A large piece of furniture for sleeping	_____
5. Food delivered to the hotel room	_____

45

4. Circle the correct word.

1. Guests meet their friends in the hotel (desk / *lobby*). [lobby circled]
2. The (key / bellman) carries the bags.
3. The (doorman / maid) signals for a taxi.
4. The (maid / clerk) cleans the hotel rooms.
5. Large hotels usually have several (luggage / elevators).
6. I sat in the (lobby / elevator) and waited for my friend.
7. The bellman expected a larger (floor / tip).
8. Call (room service / housekeeping) to order breakfast.

5. Fill in the blanks.

At the Hotel

Last weekend I went to New York City. I had already made my R _ _ _ _ _ _ _ _ I _ _ S at the Nikko Hotel. When I arrived, I C _ _ C _ _ _ _ I _ with the C _ _ _ _ standing at the F _ _ _ _ D _ _ K. She R _ G _ _ _ _ _ _ E D me and gave me a K _ _. Then the B _ _ _ M _ _ carried my L _ _ _ _ G _ upstairs to my S _ _ _ _.

6. Write the word under the appropriate category.

	PERSON	ACTION	LOCATION
ballroom			BALLROOM
check out		CHECK OUT	
clerk	CLERK		
front desk			
doorman			
elevator operator			
floor			
guest			
lobby			
lounge			
maid			
register			
reserve			
room			
suite			

7. What is the correct order for these actions? Number them from 1 to 8.

1. ____   The doorman opened the door for me.
2. ____   I registered at the front desk.
3. _1_   I arrived at the hotel.
4. ____   The bellman escorted me to the elevator.
5. ____   The elevator operator asked for my floor.
6. ____   I returned to the lobby.
7. ____   I tried the door to my suite.
8. ____   The key would not open the door.

READING PRACTICE

1. Which underlined word is incorrect? Circle the letter.

> **GRAMMAR TO KNOW:**
> conditional sentences   conjunctions
> modal auxiliaries   prepositions

1. The bellman should <u>carry</u> your luggage <u>to</u> your room if he is <u>ask</u>.
                    A   B   (C)

2. Your reservation will be <u>cancelled</u> if you <u>didn't</u> check <u>in</u> before 6 p.m.
                    A   B   C

3. Hello, I <u>will</u> like to reserve a suite <u>with</u> a double bed <u>and</u> a view.
        A   B   C

4. Please <u>call</u> the front desk if you <u>needed</u> a key <u>for</u> your guests.
          A   B   C

5. Mrs. Connors <u>also</u> Mr. Shaw met <u>in</u> the lobby to <u>discuss</u> business.
            A   B   C

6. Please <u>wait</u> in the lounge <u>but</u> the doorman <u>calls</u> you a taxicab.
       A   B   C

7. The housekeeping staff <u>does</u> their work <u>of</u> the afternoons <u>while</u> everyone
              A   B   C
   is out.

8. This hotel <u>is</u> known <u>for</u> its beautiful lobby <u>also</u> large rooms.
      A   B   C

9. The maid <u>waited</u> until the guest left <u>but</u> <u>entered</u> the room.
        A   B   C

10. If you <u>see</u> a desk clerk, <u>asked</u> him if the hotel <u>requires</u> reservations.
         A   B   C

2. Read the following conversation and answer the questions.

> Maid: Good morning. I'm from Housekeeping. May I clean the room?
> Guest: Please come in. I'm checking out now.
> Maid: In that case, I'll just leave these towels. I'll come back later and prepare the room for the next guest.
> Guest: I'll be gone in 10 minutes.

1. What time of day is it?
   (A) Morning
   (B) Afternoon
   (C) Evening

2. Why is the maid there?
   (A) To turn down the bed
   (B) To deliver breakfast
   (C) To clean the room

3. What did the maid leave?
   (A) Keys
   (B) Towels
   (C) Luggage

4. When will the guest leave?
   (A) Tomorrow morning
   (B) Later in the evening
   (C) In 10 minutes

3. Read the following paragraph and answer the questions.

> When a taxi arrives at a hotel, a doorman opens the door for the passengers. He takes their luggage and escorts them through the lobby. The bellman waits by the front desk. He shows the guests their rooms and carries their luggage.

1. Who opens the taxi door?
   (A) The driver
   (B) The passengers
   (C) The doorman

2. The doorman escorts the guests through
   (A) the dining room
   (B) the lobby
   (C) the elevator

3. Where does the bellman wait?
   (A) By the front desk
   (B) By the front door
   (C) Near the elevator

4. Who shows the guests their rooms?
   (A) The doorman
   (B) The bellman
   (C) The elevator operator

13 GARDENING AND FARMING

WORDS TO KNOW

bed	harvest	plant	seedling
bug	hose	plot	soil
bulb	insect	pot	spray
crop	insecticide	produce	sprout
dig	pest	raise	transplant
ground	pesticide	rake	water
grow	pick	seed	weed

WORD PRACTICE

1. Write the name of the tool beside the action.

CHOICES: shovel, hose, rake

ACTION	TOOL
1. To dig	SHOVEL
2. To water	_____
3. To rake leaves	_____

2. Fill in the blanks.

How to Start a Garden

Put S E E D S in the S _ _ _ . Wait a few days for them to S _ _ _ _ T . Give them plenty of W _ _ _ _ . As the sprouts G _ _ _ , keep W _ _ _ S away. Soon you will have a healthy crop of V _ _ _ _ _ _ _ _ _ .

3. Draw a line between words with similar meanings.

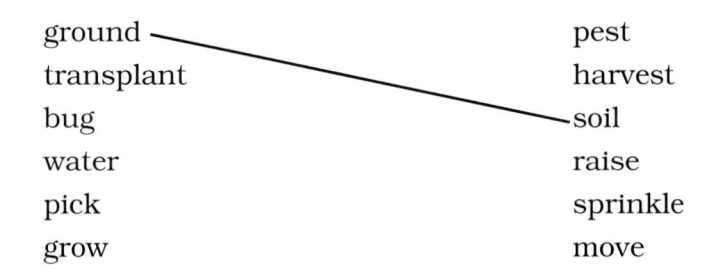

ground — pest
transplant   harvest
bug ————— soil
water   raise
pick   sprinkle
grow   move

49

4. Make progressive verbs. Add -ing to the following words.

1. spray   <u>SPRAYING</u>
2. grow   _____
3. weed   _____
4. plant   _____
5. water   _____
6. harvest   _____
7. sprout   _____

5. Write the correct -ing words from Exercise 4 in the blanks.

1. <u>G R O W I N G</u> plants need a lot of sun, water, and good soil.
2. Fall is usually the time for <u>H _ _ _ _ _ _ _ G</u> crops.
3. <u>W _ _ _ _ _ _ G</u> plants daily is good, especially in a dry environment.
4. The plants are <u>S _ _ _ _ _ _ _ G</u> early since we have had such a wet spring.
5. Frequent <u>S _ _ _ _ _ _ G</u> with insecticides will kill bugs.
6. Removing unwanted plants is called <u>W _ _ _ _ _ G</u>.
7. <u>P _ _ _ _ _ _ G</u> a garden is usually done in the spring.

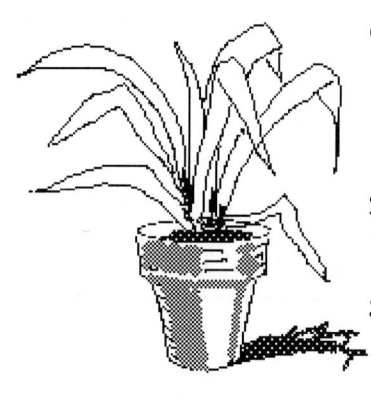

GROWING EXPRESSIONS

1. She has a green thumb. =
   She can make plants grow.

2. The corn is as tall as an elephant's eye. =
   The corn is very tall.

3. The soil is dry as a bone. =
   The plant needs water.

Reading Practice

1. Which underlined word is incorrect? Circle the letter.

> **Grammar to Know:**
> causative verbs   conjunctions
> infinitives   verb tense

1. This bed of flowers <u>will</u> <u>requiring</u> frequent <u>watering</u>.
                      A   (B)   C

2. It <u>is</u> time <u>harvesting</u> our crop <u>of</u> vegetables.
      A   B   C

3. Seedlings are <u>to begin</u> to sprout through <u>the</u> soil on <u>our</u> farm.
                 A   B   C

4. You must <u>dug</u> <u>deeply</u> <u>in order to</u> plant these bulbs.
            A   B   C

5. The tomato bug <u>ruin</u> <u>all</u> the produce <u>in</u> the county last summer.
               A   B   C

6. <u>I'd</u> like <u>grow</u> prize-winning vegetables in my garden <u>this</u> year.
   A   B   C

7. This bug <u>being</u> a common pest found <u>on</u> this type <u>of</u> plant.
           A   B   C

8. Ms. Donaldson first <u>grows</u> strong seedlings <u>while</u> she trans-
                                A   B
   plants them <u>to</u> small pots.
              C

9. I <u>had</u> Suzanne <u>raked</u> the flower bed <u>before</u> she planted more flowers.
     A   B   C

10. This plot <u>of</u> land <u>is</u> large enough <u>growing</u> an important crop.
           A   B   C

A Tractor

A tractor is used to haul farm equipment and to plow and till the soil. Special equipment can be attached to the tractor to sow seeds, to irrigate the fields, and to spray pesticides.

2. Read the following conversation and answer the questions.

> Customer: Do you have any flowers? I don't see any.
> Farmer: I didn't grow any flowers this year, only vegetables.
> Customer: I would like to buy just these green beans then. How much are they?
> Farmer: Let me weigh them. Two pounds. That's 84 cents.

1. Why doesn't the farmer sell flowers?
   (A) Because he didn't bring vases.
   (B) Because he didn't grow any.
   (C) Because they're expensive.

2. How does the farmer sell his produce?
   (A) By color
   (B) By size
   (C) By weight

3. How much is one pound of green beans?
   (A) 42 cents
   (B) 84 cents
   (C) 2 dollars

4. How many pounds did the customer buy?
   (A) 2
   (B) 4
   (C) 8

3. Read the following passage and answer the questions.

> Many gardeners today do not like to use insecticides or pesticides. They do not like chemicals in their gardens. They use natural insect controls instead. Certain flowers can keep bugs away. Some gardeners plant these flowers next to the vegetables. The flowers are a natural way to keep the vegetable healthy. They also add beauty to the garden.

1. Why don't some gardeners like chemicals?
   (A) They are not natural.
   (B) The chemicals are too weak.
   (C) The chemicals attract bugs.

2. The bugs stay away from
   (A) certain flowers
   (B) vegetables
   (C) outdoor pools

3. Where do gardeners plant these flowers?
   (A) In window boxes
   (B) Next to the vegetables
   (C) In the front yard

4. The flowers are natural and also
   (A) wild
   (B) expensive
   (C) beautiful

14 THE GAS STATION

WORDS TO KNOW

air	fill (it) up	gas tank	repair
air pump	fix	grease	spare tire
car	flat tire	hood	tire
change the oil	gas	jack	trunk
check the oil	gas pump	mechanic	wheel
engine	gas station	oil change	windshield

WORD PRACTICE

1. Complete the sentences.

1. The <u>E N G I N E</u> is located under the <u>H _ _ D</u>.
2. Make sure the <u>T _ _ _ S</u> have enough <u>A _ _</u>.
3. The <u>W _ _ _ S _ _ _ _ D</u> should be kept clean.
4. If the <u>G _ _ T _ _ K</u> is empty, <u>F _ _ L</u> it <u>_ _</u>.
5. The spare tire is in the <u>T _ _ _ _</u>.

2. Cross out the word that does NOT belong.

1. gas   oil   ~~coins~~
2. hood   paper   windshield
3. wheel   tire   rain
4. fill it up take a break check the oil
5. jack   oil   flat tire

3. Draw a line between a word and its definition.

NOUN	DEFINITION
windshield —————————— gas station
service station —————— front window of a car
gas	fix a problem
repair	car repairman
mechanic	fuel

53

4. What can a driver get for his car at a gas station? Circle the 4 words.

ink   (gas)   cream   vinegar

oil   bread   grease   air

5. Write the simple form of the verb.

1. filling up   __FILL UP__ the tank.
2. changing   _____ the oil.
3. checking   _____ the tires.
4. pumping   _____ the gas.
5. repairing   _____ the engine.

6. Circle the correct verb form.

1. I (filling the car up / (fill the car up)) with gas when the gas tank is empty.
2. The service station attendant is (changing / change) the oil now.
3. You should (check/ checking) the air pressure of your tires.
4. A service station attendant (pumps / pumping) gas for a living.
5. The mechanic is (repair / repairing) the engine today.

7. Complete the sentences.

1. I have a flat tire.

   I need to change the __TIRE__.

2. The oil is low. It's down a quart.

   I need to add some _____.

3. The oil is dirty. I haven't changed it for 15,000 miles.

   I need to _____ the oil.

4. The mechanic wants to check the oil.

   He must check under the _____.

5. I have a flat tire.

   The spare one is in the _____.

8. Label the parts of the car.

CHOICES: hood, tire, trunk, windshield

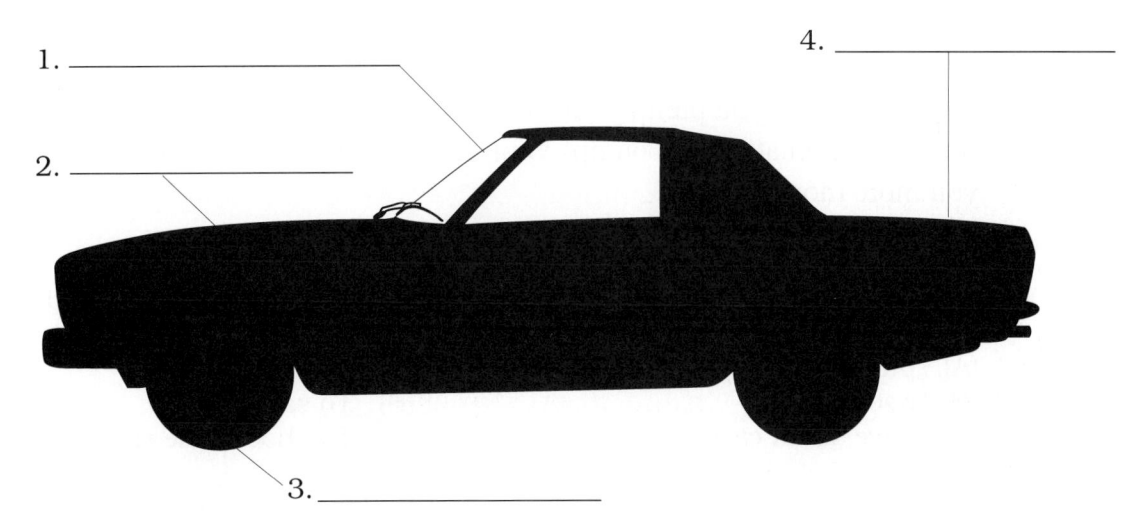

1. _____
2. _____
3. _____
4. _____

READING PRACTICE

1. Which underlined word is incorrect? Circle the letter.

> **GRAMMAR TO KNOW:**
> infinitives   adverbs of frequency
> modal auxiliaries   subject-verb agreement

1. To prevent <u>a</u> flat tire, you <u>do</u> put air in your tires <u>regularly</u>.
                A   (B)   C

2. Lori took <u>the</u> car <u>to</u> the gas station <u>filling</u> it up.
            A   B   C

3. Steven <u>used</u> the jack to raise the tire <u>off</u> the ground <u>changing</u> it.
         A   B   C

4. Marilyn <u>once a week</u> checks <u>the</u> oil in <u>her</u> car.
           A   B   C

5. The mechanic <u>walk</u> up to <u>the</u> gas pump to <u>help</u> the customer.
         A   B   C

6. If <u>your</u> car needs repair, you <u>will have</u> ask a mechanic <u>for</u> help.
      A   B   C

7. Bill opened <u>the</u> hood of the car <u>seeing</u> what was wrong <u>with</u> the engine.
          A   B   C

8. There <u>are</u> a spare tire <u>in</u> the trunk <u>of</u> my car.
      A   B   C

9. There <u>are</u> grease <u>on</u> the engine <u>of</u> my car.
      A   B   C

10. The tires <u>of</u> my old car <u>once a year</u> need <u>to be</u> replaced.
        A   B   C

2. Read the following paragraph and answer the questions.

> Many service station customers today pump their own gas. This is a recent change. A few years ago, a service station attendant would put gas in your car, check the oil, and clean your windshield. Now, if you pump your own gas, you save money. If a service station attendant pumps your gas or checks your oil, it costs you more money.

1. Many customers at gas stations today
   (A) pump their own gas
   (B) use less gas
   (C) have small cars

2. What does the station attendant do to your oil?
   (A) Checks it
   (B) Cooks with it
   (C) Pumps it

3. Why do customers pump their own gas?
   (A) To learn how
   (B) To save money
   (C) To choose the right gas

4. When did customers start pumping their own gas?
   (A) Only recently
   (B) In the summer
   (C) During vacation

3. Read the following conversation and answer the questions.

> Station Attendant: Your car needed oil. We put in a quart of oil.
> Customer: Is that the only problem? I was afraid it was something more serious.
> Station Attendant: Everything seems OK. Make sure that the oil doesn't get too low.
> Customer: I won't. How much do I owe you?
> Station Attendant: $12.50 plus 1.42 tax. That's $13.92 total.

1. What was the problem with the car?
   (A) It was old.
   (B) It needed oil.
   (C) It was out of gas.

2. What will the customer do next?
   (A) Repair the car
   (B) Add oil
   (C) Pay the bill

3. How much oil did the attendant put in the car?
   (A) A gallon
   (B) A quart
   (C) An ounce

4. How much was the tax?
   (A) $12.50
   (B) $13.92
   (C) $1.42

15 THE MILITARY

WORDS TO KNOW

airfield	duty	off-duty	serve
Air Force	enlist	on-duty	service
Army	fly	officer	soldier
barracks	infantry	parade	stripe
base	inspection	pilot	submarine
camp	march	rank	tank
Coast Guard	Marines	recruit	tour
combat	mess hall	reserves	troops
draft	military	rifle	uniform
drill	Navy	sailor	veteran

WORD PRACTICE

1. Write the words that are defined below.

1. to walk in military formation: M A R C H
2. where soldiers sleep: B _ _ _ _ _ _ S
3. underwater ship: S _ _ M A R _ _ E
4. a soldier's clothing: U _ _ _ _ _ M
5. groups of soldiers: T _ _ _ P S
6. military practice: D _ _ _ L

2. Idiom practice: fill in the blanks with words from the list above.

1. A military person is " in the S E R V I C E."
2. A soldier at work is " on D _ _ Y."
3. A military person in official clothes is " in U _ _ F _ _ M."
4. A soldier away from the army camp is " off B _ _ E."
5. Soldiers fighting are "in C _ _ B _ T."

57

3. Write the *-ing* form of these verbs to complete these sentences.

VERBS   SENTENCES

1. fly   The pilots are _____ the jets.
2. drill   The new recruits are tired of _____ .
3. enlist   The students are thinking about _____ in the Army.
4. inspect   The sergeant is _____ the barracks.
5. sail   The ship is _____ this evening.
6. march   The soldiers are _____ on the field.
7. recruit   The officers are _____ pilots for the Air Force.
8. join   The woman is _____ the Army.

4. Draw a line between military words and their general meanings.

mess hall	practice
drill	dormitory
base	clothes
uniform	fighting
combat	"town"
barracks	dining room

5. Write the word under the appropriate category.

	PERSON	TYPE OF TRANSPORTATION	PLACE
veteran	VETERAN		
submarine		SUBMARINE	
soldier			
officer			
mess hall			MESS HALL
camp			
tank			
barracks			

Reading Practice

1. Which underlined word is incorrect? Circle the letter.

> **Grammar to Know:**
> modal auxiliaries   conjunctions
> subject-verb agreement   prepositions

1. My uncle <u>was recruited</u> <u>in</u> the Army <u>and</u> served a 15-year military career.
                 A   Ⓑ   C

2. <u>In</u> the Navy most sailors <u>are expected</u> to serve <u>at</u> a submarine.
     A   B   C

3. <u>Most</u> personnel who enlist <u>in</u> the Air Force <u>will</u> like to fly jets.
     A   B   C

4. The troops <u>marched</u> past the mess hall <u>while</u> returned <u>to</u> the barracks.
              A   B   C

5. Today's parade <u>included</u> veterans <u>but</u> reserve officers <u>as well as</u> troops in uniform.
           A   B   C

6. Soldiers <u>must</u> <u>drill</u> for combat with rifles <u>also</u> tanks.
        A B   C

7. <u>The</u> third infantry unit <u>hope</u> to pass <u>inspection</u> this morning.
    A   B   C

8. Whether they <u>are</u> on-duty or off-duty, the soldiers must <u>been</u> <u>in</u> uniform.
            A   B C

9. To avoid <u>being</u> drafted <u>into</u> the Army, many men <u>enlists</u> in the Navy.
       A   B   C

10. The Air Force <u>practice</u> drills <u>on</u> the airfield <u>all</u> day.
             A   B   C

Everyday Expressions with Military Terms

1. Anchors aweigh. = Let's get going.

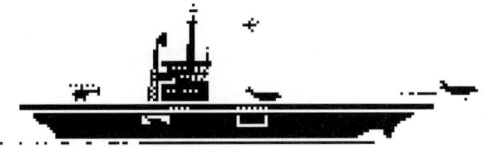

2. This place is like boot camp. =
   This place demands a lot of hard work.

3. SNAFU =
   Situation Normal; All Fouled Up.

59

2. Read the following paragraph and answer the questions.

> More than twenty years ago, all eighteen-year-old men registered for military service. This registration was part of "the draft." If you were drafted, you were conscripted into the Army. About twenty years ago, this "draft" system was discontinued. Today the army is composed almost entirely of volunteers.

1. Today the army is made up of
   (A) draftees
   (B) volunteers
   (C) officers

2. When was the draft last used?
   (A) 8 years ago
   (B) About 20 years ago
   (C) 100 years ago

3. At what age did men register for the draft?
   (A) 18
   (B) 19
   (C) 20

4. Which of the following is true of the draft system?
   (A) It's no longer in use.
   (B) It's a volunteer organization.
   (C) It's only for men under 18.

3. Read the following conversation and answer the questions.

> Luke: Were you in the Army?
> Mark: Yes, I was drafted twenty years ago.
> Luke: I was in the Navy, but I enlisted.
> Mark: My brother was a sailor, too.
> Luke: Actually, I was a Navy pilot.

1. How did Mark join the Army?
   (A) He volunteered.
   (B) He signed up.
   (C) He was drafted.

2. What did Luke enlist in?
   (A) The Army
   (B) The Navy
   (C) The Air Force

3. Mark's brother was a
   (A) sailor
   (B) pilot
   (C) marine

4. What was Luke's job in the Navy?
   (A) Sailor
   (B) Pilot
   (C) Admiral

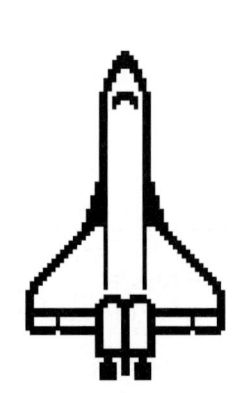

ASTRONAUTS

Separate from the Army, Navy, and Air Force is NASA, the National Aeronautic and Space Administration.

NASA operates the Space Shuttle and sends astronauts to outer space.

The word *astronauts* means "sailors of the stars."

16 THE POLICE AND THE LAW

WORDS TO KNOW

arrest	guard	police car	suspicion
attorney	handcuffs	policeman	testify
case	imprison	police officer	testimony
cell	jail	police station	thief
court	judge	policewoman	trial
crime	jury	prison	try
criminal	lawyer	prisoner	victim
defendant	misdemeanor	prosecutor	violate
defense	officer	robber	violation
felony	patrol	sentence	violator
fine	patrol car	suspect	witness

WORD PRACTICE

1. Draw a line between words that are similar in meaning.

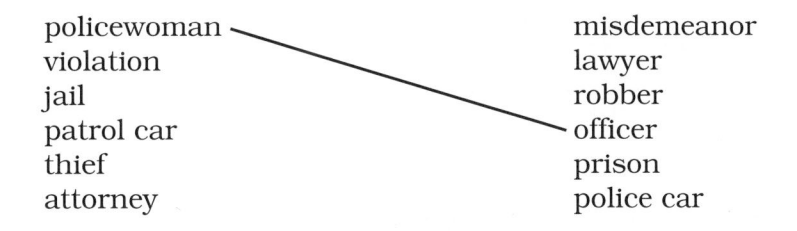

policewoman — misdemeanor
violation — lawyer
jail — robber
patrol car — officer
thief — prison
attorney — police car

2. Write the noun for the *person*.

PLACE OR ACT   PERSON

1. robbery   The ROBBER stole the camera.
2. crime   The _____ was sent to jail.
3. prosecution   The _____ won the case.
4. judgement   The _____ sentenced the criminal.
5. theft   The _____ picked my pocket.
6. prison   The _____ waited in her cell.

POLICE OFFICER'S BADGE

This badge represents the authority of the police officer. It is used for identification. (The word "identification" is often shortened to ID. The badge is a police officer's ID.)

3. Past Tense Review: Add *-d* or *-ed* to the following verbs.

1. jail   JAILED
2. sentence   _____
3. book   _____
4. arrest   _____
5. imprison   _____
6. judge   _____
7. witness   _____

4. Write the Simple Present Tense of the verb in the sentences below.

1. A person ____TESTIFIES____ under oath.
   (*testify*)
2. Someone always _____ a public crime.
   (*witness*)
3. Society _____ no one without a trial.
   (*judge*)
4. A judge _____ criminals found guilty.
   (*sentence*)
5. A police officer _____ criminals.
   (*arrest*)

5. Write the noun form of the verb. Some may have two forms.

VERB	NOUN
1. to suspect	SUSPECT / SUSPICION
2. to testify	_____
3. to violate	_____
4. to imprison	_____
5. to prosecute	_____
6. to defend	_____
7. to rob	_____

READING PRACTICE

1. Which underlined word is incorrect? Circle the letter.

> **GRAMMAR TO KNOW:**
> adjective comparisons   infinitives
> conditional sentences   two-word verbs

1. The suspect was arrested <u>and</u> charged <u>for</u> a crime he had <u>never</u>
                                 A   (B)   C
   committed.

2. The policewoman <u>was off-duty</u> when she came <u>across</u> the <u>worse</u>
                    A   B   C
   accident she had ever seen.

3. If <u>the</u> suspect wishes, <u>he</u> can <u>had</u> a lawyer represent him.
       A   B   C

4. The prosecutor <u>called</u> the witness <u>up</u> before the jury <u>testify</u>.
                  A   B   C

5. <u>The</u> defendant was <u>brought out</u> her jail cell <u>into</u> the courtroom.
    A   B   C

6. Because Mr. Simon committed <u>a</u> felony, he was forced <u>wearing</u> handcuffs
                                    A   B
   <u>to</u> his trial.
   C

7. The judge reviewed <u>the</u> case <u>and</u> pronounced <u>longest</u> jail sentence allowed
                        A   B   C
   by the law.

8. The prisoner <u>attempted</u> <u>grab</u> the gun <u>from</u> the guard.
                A   B   C

9. <u>The</u> defense lawyer <u>went</u> to <u>look of</u> the important file.
    A   B   C

10. If you refuse <u>to pay</u> your traffic ticket, you <u>would</u> have to go <u>to</u> court.
                 A   B   C

JUDICIAL SYMBOL

This is the symbol of the law. It represents the balance between right and wrong.

2. Read the following conversation and answer the questions.

> Man: Officer! Officer! This woman robbed me! She's a thief!
> Woman: He's crazy. Arrest him. Put handcuffs on him. Put him in jail and throw away the key.
> Man: Don't listen to her. I want my attorney. She took my watch. I have witnesses. They'll testify at the trial.
> Woman: You left your watch at home, moron.
> Officer: Are you two husband and wife?
> Woman: Of course! Do you think I would talk to this man otherwise?
> Man: She's a liar. A convicted felon. Don't listen to her.

1. What did the man accuse the woman of?
   (A) Robbing him
   (B) Stealing a car
   (C) Selling his watch

2. What does the woman suggest the officer do to the man?
   (A) Give him a ride
   (B) Ask him his age
   (C) Put him in jail

3. Where did the man leave his watch?
   (A) At the police station
   (B) At home
   (C) At the trial

4. The man and woman are
   (A) lost
   (B) married
   (C) guilty

3. Read the following paragraph and answer the questions.

> A judge presides over a court trial. The prosecuting attorney presents the case for the victim. The lawyer for the defense presents the case for the defendant. The jury listens to the arguments. The twelve people on the jury decide whether the defendant is guilty or not guilty.
>
> If the defendant is guilty, he or she will be sentenced by the judge. The judge can fine the criminal (for example, a $12,000 fine) or can send him or her to jail.

1. Who presides over a trial?
   (A) A judge
   (B) A defendant
   (C) A victim

2. Who decides "guilty" or "innocent"?
   (A) The victim
   (B) The jury
   (C) The judge

3. How many people are usually on a jury?
   (A) Only the judge
   (B) Two
   (C) Twelve

4. Who sentences a criminal?
   (A) The jury
   (B) The prosecutor
   (C) The judge

17 ARTISTS

WORDS TO KNOW

brush	drawing	medium	sculpture
can	easel	oil	show
canvas	exhibition	painting	sketch
carve	frame	palette	still life
clay	gallery	paper	stone
collection	ink	pencil	tube
color	landscape	portrait	watercolor
draw	media	potter	wood

WORD PRACTICE

1. Cross out the word that does NOT belong with the first word.

1. color: blue   orange   ~~old~~
2. draw: pencil   chair   pen
3. paint: lamp   oil   watercolor
4. carve: stone   book   wood
5. collection: gallery   museum   television
6. painting: portrait   house   landscape

2. Complete the questions.

1. Question: What is an E A S E L ?
   Answer: A wooden tripod that holds a canvas

2. Question: What is a P _ _ _ _ E ?
   Answer: A flat object on which paints are mixed

3. Question: What is a T _ _ E ?
   Answer: A container for oil paints

4. Question: What is a S _ _ _ _   L _ _ _ ?
   Answer: A painting of objects on a table

5. Question: What is a L _ _ _ _ _ _ E ?
   Answer: A painting of outdoor scenery

65

3. Write the Present Tense form of the Verb.

	PRESENT	PAST
1.	DRAW	drew
2.	_____	painted
3.	_____	carved
4.	_____	framed
5.	_____	showed

4. Complete the sentences using the appropriate Past Tense of the verbs in Exercise 2.

1. The artist D R E W a picture with a pencil.

2. Many artists S H _ _ _ _ their work in the exhibition.

3. The framer F _ _ _ _ _ the watercolor.

4. Many famous artists P _ _ _ _ _ _ portraits.

5. The sculptor C _ _ _ _ _ the statue out of stone.

5. Fill in the blanks.

An Artist at Work

When an artist paints, he or she places the C A N V A S on an E _ _ _ L. The artist may S _ _ _ _ _ H an idea on the canvas before starting to P _ _ _ _. An artist might paint with O _ _ S or with W _ _ _ R _ _ _ O R S.

66

6. Write the noun form of the following verbs.

VERB	NOUN (inanimate)	NOUN (animate)
1. exhibit	EXHIBITION	EXHIBITOR
2. collect	_____	_____
3. paint	_____	_____
4. sculpt	_____	_____

READING PRACTICE

1. Which underlined word is incorrect? Circle the letter.

> **GRAMMAR TO KNOW:**
> conditional sentences   gerunds
> prepositions   infinitives

1. An artist <u>mixes</u> paints <u>on</u> the palette rather than <u>at</u> the canvas.
          A   B   (C)

2. This painter <u>is</u> <u>to know</u> more for his portrait work <u>than</u> for his landscapes.
                 A B   C

3. Sheila prefers <u>paint</u> with oils <u>rather</u> <u>than</u> watercolors.
                A   B   C

4. If you <u>like</u> sculpture, <u>gone</u> to the sculpture gallery <u>on</u> 7th Street.
          A   B   C

5. A <u>great</u> artist <u>needs</u> only paper and a pencil <u>creating</u> a masterpiece.
       A   B   C

6. The <u>painting</u> instructor keeps <u>all</u> the brushes <u>into</u> a can.
           A   B   C

7. It <u>is</u> best not <u>using</u> an easel when <u>working</u> with watercolors.
      A   B   C

8. If you <u>like</u> Matisse, you should <u>going</u> to <u>see</u> the exhibit at the museum.
          A   B   C

9. My new collection <u>consists</u> mainly <u>in</u> ink <u>drawings</u>.
                       A   B   C

10. Many ancient sculptors <u>used</u> clay or marble <u>carving</u> portraits <u>of</u> heroes.
                            A   B   C

2. Read the following paragraph and answer the questions.

> The art store has everything for the artist. Artists work in many media: painters may work in watercolor, ink, pencil, or oils; potters may work in clay; sculptors may work in stone or wood. Whatever the medium, the art store has the supplies.

1. Where can an artist find supplies?
   (A) At a museum
   (B) At an art school
   (C) At an art store

2. Which of the following is NOT mentioned as an art medium?
   (A) Stone
   (B) Radio
   (C) Oils

3. Who works in clay?
   (A) Potters
   (B) Gallery owners
   (C) Painters

4. Which media do sculptors use?
   (A) Pen and ink
   (B) Stone and wood
   (C) Clay and oils

3. Read the following conversation and answer the questions.

> Guide: The exhibition in this gallery is the museum's collection of watercolors.
> Visitor: Are there any pen and ink drawings in the collection?
> Guide: Yes. They're on the third floor.
> Visitor Will we tour the sculpture garden?
> Guide: Yes. The stone sculptures are outside in the garden. The wood ones are inside the museum.

1. What is the exhibition of?
   (A) Watercolor
   (B) Oils
   (C) Pottery

2. Where are the pen and ink drawings?
   (A) On the lower level
   (B) In the garden
   (C) On the third floor

3. Where is the tour taking place?
   (A) In a museum
   (B) On a bus
   (C) In the park

4. Where are wood sculptures kept?
   (A) In the forest
   (B) Inside the museum
   (C) In the sculpture garden

THE MONA LISA

The *Mona Lisa* by Leonardo da Vinci is one of the most famous paintings in the world. It hangs in the Louvre Museum in Paris. The *Mona Lisa* is known for her smile.

18 BANKS

WORDS TO KNOW

balance	checkbook	fee	savings account
bank slip	checking account	interest	service charge
bank statement	credit cards	lend	teller
borrow	currency	loan	teller window
cash	debt	percent	transaction
check	deposit	receipt	withdrawal

WORD PRACTICE

1. Write the words under the appropriate category.

teller
currency
bank manager
interest

checkbook
service charge
cash
bank slip

deposit slip
customer
withdrawal slip
balance

PEOPLE
TELLER

MONEY
CURRENCY

FORM
CHECKBOOK

2. Use the words from the Words To Know section to complete the sentences.

1. People can write checks to pay for their purchases if there is money in their _C_ _H_ _ _ _ _ _ _ account.

2. One service of a bank is _L_ _E_ _ _ _ _ _G_ money.

3. _B_ _ _ _K_ _ _ _ hours are usually from 9 am to 2 pm.

4. Identification is required when _C_ _ _ _H_ _ _ _ _ a check.

5. _W_ _ _T_ _H_ _ _ _ _ _ _I_ _N_ _G_ money from your account will reduce your savings.

6. _B_ _ _ _ _ _ _ _E_ _D_ money must be repaid.

7. Consumers often pay for purchases with bank _C_ _ _ _ _ _T_ _C_ _ _ _S_ .

69

3. Look at this bank statement and answer the questions.

1st Federal Bank	Statement	April, 1991
John Doe	CHECKING ACCOUNT	
	Balance Last Month	+ 642.00
4/09/91	Deposit	+ 106.00
4/09/91	Check #432	- 4.75
4/10/91	Check #433	- 13.00
4/20/91	Service Charge	- 40.00
4/21/91	Deposit	+ 208.00
4/22/91	Interest	+ 6.42
4/30/91	Balance	904.67

1. How many checks were written in April? _____
2. What was last month's balance? _____
3. What is the balance for April? _____
4. How much interest was added to the account? _____
5. How much was the service charge? _____

4. Fill in the blanks.

To put money in the bank, fill out a D _ _ _ _ _ I slip. To take money out of a bank, fill out a W _ _ D _ _ _ _ L slip. Take the slips to the T _ _ L E R. The teller stands behind the T E _ _ _ _ _ _ W _ _ D O _. The teller will give you your B _ _ _ _ _ _ after your T R A N S _ _ _ _ _ _.

5. Look at this check and answer the questions.

```
                                                    546
1st Federal Bank    Oct 5, 1991
Pay to the Order of   District Loan Co.      $ 55.00
Sum  Fifty-five and •••••• 00/100 dollars
Memo: Car Loan Payment                        J Doe
```

1. Who wrote the check? _____
2. To whom was the check written? _____
3. When was the check written? _____
4. How much was the check for? _____
5. What is the check for? _____
6. What is the check number? _____

6. Draw a line between opposites.

cash ——————————————— customer
teller ——————————————— check
deposit   service charge
interest   borrow
lend   withdrawal

7. Write the *-ing* form of the following verbs.

1. cash   _____CASHING_____
2. lend   _____
3. withdraw _____
4. check   _____
5. bank   _____
6. borrow   _____

READING PRACTICE

1. Which underlined word is incorrect?

> **GRAMMAR TO KNOW:**
> conditional sentences   gerunds
> prepositions   infinitives

1. If you would like <u>to</u> make <u>a</u> deposit, you must <u>filled</u> out a bank slip.
                 A   B   (C)

2. There <u>is</u> a small service charge <u>for</u> <u>cashed</u> a check.
      A   B   C

3. Would you like <u>making</u> a withdrawal <u>from</u> <u>your</u> savings account?
                  A   B   C

4. There <u>is</u> a high rate <u>in</u> interest <u>on</u> this loan.
      A   B   C

5. If you <u>are</u> in debt, this bank will <u>lent</u> you money <u>at</u> a rate of eight percent.
          A   B   C

6. Your balance <u>will</u> be <u>displayed</u> <u>at</u> your deposit receipt.
              A   B   C

7. The teller <u>said</u> I should <u>contact</u> the branch manager <u>inquire</u> about loans.
           A   B   C

8. There <u>is</u> a penalty <u>to</u> early withdrawal <u>from</u> this account.
      A   B   C

9. Joan tried <u>balanced</u> her checkbook and <u>realized</u> that she had <u>lost</u> a check.
           A   B   C

10. When you drive <u>in</u> to the teller window, <u>ask</u> the teller <u>for</u> a bank slip.
                  A   B   C

2. Read the following conversation and answer the questions.

Customer:	I need a loan. I want to buy a house.
Bank officer:	Do you have any debts?
Customer:	I have a $3,000 car loan and a $10,000 school loan.
Bank officer:	How much do you want to borrow?
Customer:	Can you lend me $100,000?

1. What does the customer want?
   - (A) A withdrawal slip
   - (B) A savings account
   - (C) A loan

2. Why does the customer need money?
   - (A) She wants to buy a house.
   - (B) She needs a new car.
   - (C) She wants to go to school.

3. How many loans does the customer have?
   - (A) 1
   - (B) 2
   - (C) 3

4. How much does she want to borrow?
   - (A) $3,000
   - (B) $10,000
   - (C) $100,000

3. Read the following paragraph and answer the questions.

A checking account is convenient. You can easily pay your bills with checks. Your paycheck can be deposited into your checking account directly. Many people prefer to keep their money in a savings account because a savings account earns interest. This interest can be between 5% to 8% or more. A checking account usually does not offer interest.

1. What is good about a checking account?
   - (A) It is profitable.
   - (B) It is convenient.
   - (C) It is free.

2. Why do some people prefer savings accounts?
   - (A) They have little money.
   - (B) They hate checks.
   - (C) They like to receive interest.

3. What can be deposited into a checking account?
   - (A) A bill
   - (B) A paycheck
   - (C) A service charge

4. How high can interest be?
   - (A) Only 8%
   - (B) Less than 8%
   - (C) More than 8%

FORMS OF MONEY

| Credit Card | Bills | Coins |

19 TRAVEL

WORDS TO KNOW

airport	driver	section	runway
air traffic control	economy class	on time	smoking
arrival	express	one way	steward
board	first class	overhead bin	stewardess
bus	flight	passenger	tail
bus station	flight attendant	passport	take off
car	gate	pilot	taxi
coach	hand luggage	plane	ticket agent
control tower	jet	platform	track
customs	land	port	train
departure	local	reservation clerk	train station
dining car	nonsmoking	round trip	wing

WORD PRACTICE

1. Word Family: Write the noun form of the verb.

VERB   NOUN

1. fly   The _____FLIGHT_____ to Paris leaves at noon.

2. depart   Our _____ has been delayed an hour.

3. dine   The _____ car opens at 6 p.m.

4. arrive   The _____ of Flight 56 is delayed.

5. reserve   We made a _____ in first class.

6. smoke   This is the _____ section.

7. drive   The bus _____ helped load the luggage.

2. Draw a line between words that are opposites.

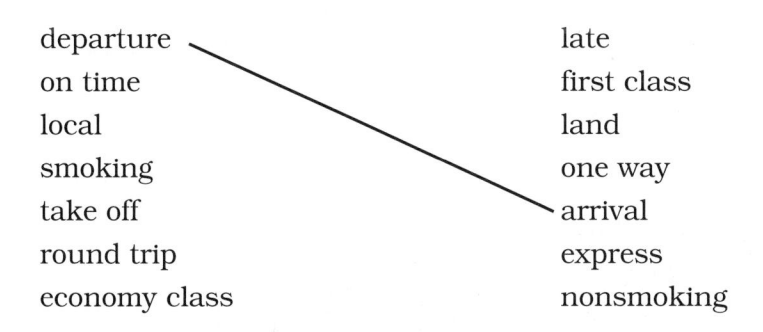

departure   late
on time   first class
local   land
smoking   one way
take off   arrival
round trip   express
economy class   nonsmoking

73

3. Complete the sentences.

1. Before boarding a plane, we line up at the G A T E .
2. For international travel, a P _ _ _ P _ _ T is necessary.
3. To get on a train, we wait on the P L _ _ F _ _ M .
4. A train runs on a T _ _ _ _ .
5. International travelers must pass through C _ _ T _ _ S .

4. Cross out the word that does NOT belong.

1. taxi — ~~smoking~~ — plane — bus
2. passenger — pilot — lawyer — flight attendant
3. tail — wing — engine — station
4. passport — dining car — customs — luggage
5. station — airport — bus stop — coins
6. luggage — late — early — on time

5. Write the word under the appropriate category.
Some words may be used more than once.

	AIRPLANE	TRAIN	BUS
airport	AIRPORT		
bus station			BUS STATION
dining car		DINING CAR	
driver			
express (2)			
flight			
jet			
pilot			
plane			
platform (2)			
runway			
take off			
train station			
wing			

6. Write the job title next to the job description.

	JOB TITLE	JOB DESCRIPTION
1.	TICKET AGENT	A person who sells tickets
2.	_____	A person in the air traffic control tower who helps a plane land
3.	_____	A person who makes travel reservations
4.	_____	A person who drives a bus
5.	_____	A person who helps passengers during a flight

READING PRACTICE

1. Which underlined word is incorrect? Circle the letter.

> **GRAMMAR TO KNOW:**
> infinitives   prepositions
> subject-verb agreement verb tense

1. Pick up <u>your</u> luggage at baggage claim before you <u>went</u> <u>through</u> customs.
          A   (B) C

2. I <u>would</u> like <u>buying</u> a one-way first class ticket <u>to</u> Denver.
     A   B   C

3. The train <u>to</u> Rome and Naples <u>are</u> <u>on</u> Track 4 right now!
         A   B C

4. <u>Please</u> <u>stowing</u> your hand luggage <u>in</u> the overhead bin.
     A   B   C

5. You should <u>has</u> your passport ready <u>as</u> you <u>board</u> the plane.
            A   B C

6. Jeff will <u>pick</u> you <u>up</u> <u>of</u> the bus station.
         A   B C

7. The pilot will <u>informed</u> us <u>of</u> local weather as we <u>land</u>.
         A   B   C

8. If you wish to <u>smoking</u>, please <u>sit</u> in <u>the</u> smoking section.
         A   B C

9. The flight attendant <u>told</u> us that <u>our</u> flight had been <u>cancel</u>.
       A   B   C

10. Please <u>tell</u> the ticket agent we <u>needs</u> two round trip tickets <u>to</u> Brussels.
      A   B   C

2. Read the following passage and answer the questions.

> One good way to see a country is to travel by bus. It isn't expensive. You can get off the bus when you feel like it, eat local food, meet local people, look around, and get on another bus later. You can also see a lot of the country by train. Most trains have dining cars, and people are always eager to meet one another.

1. Travelling by bus isn't
   (A) comfortable
   (B) expensive
   (C) good

2. What kind of food can you eat on a bus trip?
   (A) Local
   (B) Expensive
   (C) Fancy

3. Where are dining cars found?
   (A) On trains
   (B) On buses
   (C) On trucks

4. Where are people eager to meet one another?
   (A) In hotels
   (B) On trains
   (C) At the movies

3. Read the following conversation and answer the questions.

> Flight Attendant: You're in seat 3J, sir. In first class.
> Passenger: Is that seat in the smoking section?
> Flight Attendant: No, sir. This is a nonsmoking flight.
> Passenger: What time do we land in Tokyo?
> Flight Attendant: Flight time is approximately 14 hours. If we take off on time, we will land around 3:15 p.m.
> Passenger: Will my hand luggage fit in the overhead bin?
> Flight Attendant: If not, try under your seat.

1. Where is the passenger sitting?
   (A) In first class
   (B) In economy
   (C) In the smoking section

2. What are they travelling on?
   (A) A plane
   (B) A bus
   (C) A train

3. What is the passenger's destination?
   (A) Honolulu
   (B) Hong Kong
   (C) Tokyo

4. How long is the flight?
   (A) 3 hours
   (B) 14 hours
   (C) 15 hours

20 TRAINS

WORDS TO KNOW

arrive	express	passenger	snack bar
board	fare	platform	station
coach car	gate	reservation	ticket
conductor	local	reserve	timetable
depart	luggage	round trip	track
dining car	luggage rack	schedule	trip
engineer	one-way	seat	waiting room

WORD PRACTICE

1. Complete the questions.

1. Question: What is an E N G I N E E R ?
   Answer: This person sits in the locomotive and drives the train.

2. Question: What is a C _ _ _ _ _ _ _ R ?
   Answer: This person takes tickets on the train.

3. Question: What are P _ _ _ _ _ _ _ R S ?
   Answer: These people ride the train.

4. Question: What is a T _ _ _ _ _ _ _ _ ?
   Answer: This is a schedule of arrival and departure times.

5. Question: What is a T _ _ _ K ?
   Answer: This is a metal rail that trains run on.

2. Fill in the blanks.

On the Train

You can B O A R D a train after you buy a T _ _ _ _ T. After the train leaves the station, a C _ _ _ _ _ _ _ R will ask you for your T _ _ _ _ T. On the train, you can usually get something to eat at the S _ _ _ _ B _ _ in the club car or in the D _ _ _ _ _ C _ _ .

3. Write the simple form of the following -ing forms.

1. departing   DEPART
2. travelling   _____
3. reserving   _____
4. arriving   _____
5. boarding   _____

4. Write the word under the appropriate category.

	PERSON	ACTION	THING
arrive		ARRIVE	
board			
conductor	CONDUCTOR		
depart			
engineer			
reservation			RESERVATION
passenger			
ticket			
reserve			
timetable			

5. Complete the sentences.

1. I want to take the train to New York on Monday and return on Tuesday.

   I will buy a R O U N D T R I P ticket.

2. The local stops at every station. I want a faster train.

   I'll take the E _ _ _ _ _ train.

3. You can sit anywhere in the coach car.

   The seats are not R _ _ _ _ _ D.

4. If you want a big dinner, you can eat in the dining car.

   If you are not very hungry, you can eat in the S _ _ _ _ B _ _.

5. On the train you can put your luggage in the luggage rack.

   The L _ _ _ _ _ _ R _ _ _ is usually over your S _ _ _.

6. Write the word defined.

CHOICES: board, seat, schedule, passengers, gate, fare

1. train riders   PASSENGERS
2. price of a ride
3. list of times
4. get on the train
5. entry to the platform
6. place to sit

78

7. Word Family. Write the appropriate form of the underlined word.

VERB	NOUN
arrive	arrival
depart	departure
reserve	reservation
board	boarding

1. The train <u>arrives</u> at 9:45.

   _____ARRIVAL_____ time is 9:45.

2. The train _____ at 10:00.

   <u>Departure</u> time is 10:00.

3. I <u>reserved</u> seats in the club car.

   I have a _____ in the club car.

4. We will _____ the train though Gate 6.

   <u>Boarding</u> is through Gate 6.

Reading Practice

1. Which underlined word is incorrect?

GRAMMAR TO KNOW:	
conjunctions	prepostions
subject-verb agreement	verb tense

1. When you <u>travel</u> by train, you <u>may</u> <u>ate</u> in the snack bar.
                   A   B Ⓒ
2. What <u>are</u> the fare <u>for</u> a round trip ticket <u>to</u> New York?
          A   B   C
3. The local train <u>will</u> stop <u>at</u> every station, <u>still</u> the express will not.
                    A   B   C
4. <u>In</u> the coach car, you can <u>put</u> your luggage <u>of</u> the overhead luggage rack.
     A   B   C
5. Please <u>stays</u> <u>in</u> your seat so the conductor can <u>collect</u> your ticket.
            A B   C
6. We will <u>departed</u> Boston <u>at</u> 2:15 and arrive <u>in</u> New York at 4:20.
          A   B   C
7. <u>Looks</u> at the train timetable to <u>find out</u> what track your train will <u>be</u> on.
     A   B   C
8. The conductor will <u>tell</u> us when the train <u>is</u> about to <u>departing</u>.
             A   B   C
9. If the train does not <u>arrive</u> on schedule, you can <u>wait</u> <u>of</u> the waiting room.
            A   B C
10. If you <u>are</u> going <u>on</u> an overnight trip, you should always <u>calling</u> to reserve
         A   B   C
    your seat.

2. Read the following passage and answer the questions.

> Over a million people a day pass through Grand Central Station. The passengers can buy their tickets from the ticket agents, from a ticket machine, or from the conductor on the train.
>
> The passengers may wait in the waiting room for their trains. When the train is in the station, they pass through a gate to the train platform. They can board the train from the platform.
>
> On the train they can sit in the coach car (economy class) or club (first class). They can eat in the dining car or have a snack at the snack bar.

1. Where can passengers NOT buy their tickets?
   (A) From ticket agents
   (B) From the conductor
   (C) From soda machines

2. Where can passengers wait for a train?
   (A) In their hotel room
   (B) In a waiting room
   (C) In the coach car

3. Travellers in economy class will sit in
   (A) the club car
   (B) the coach car
   (C) the engine

4. Quick, short meals are available
   (A) at the snack bar
   (B) in the coach car
   (C) on the sidewalk

3. Read the following conversation and answer the questions.

> Passenger: Excuse me. Does this train stop at the Savoy station?
> Conductor: No, we go through that station. This is an express train. We don't stop there.
> Passenger: Oh, no! What should I do?
> Conductor: Get off at the next station which is Proctor City. You can get on the local train there.

1. Where does this conversation take place?
   (A) In a station
   (B) On a train
   (C) At a bus stop

2. Where does the passenger want to go?
   (A) To the end of the line
   (B) To Proctor City
   (C) To Savoy

3. Which train should the passenger have taken?
   (A) An express train
   (B) A local train
   (C) A night train

4. Where can the passenger catch the local?
   (A) Proctor City
   (B) In Savoy
   (C) Anywhere

21 CARS

WORDS TO KNOW

accelerator	engine	license plate	start
antenna	fill up	motor	station wagon
back up	fuel	passenger seat	steer
battery	gas	radiator	steering wheel
brake	gas tank	radio	taillight
brake light	glove compartment	rearview mirror	tire
bumper	headlight	reverse	trunk
convertible	hood	seat belt	turn signal
dashboard	hubcap	sedan	wheel
drive	ignition	spare tire	windshield
driver's seat	jack	speedometer	windshield wiper

WORD PRACTICE

1. Write the words that are found on the exterior of a car.

  1. H _ _ _ L _ _ _ T S
  2. W _ _ D S _ _ _ _ D   W _ _ _ R S
  3. T _ _ E S
  4. W _ _ _ L S
  5. B _ _ _ _ R S
  6. T _ _ L L _ _ _ T S

2. Draw a line between nouns that together make a new compound noun. Write the compound noun.

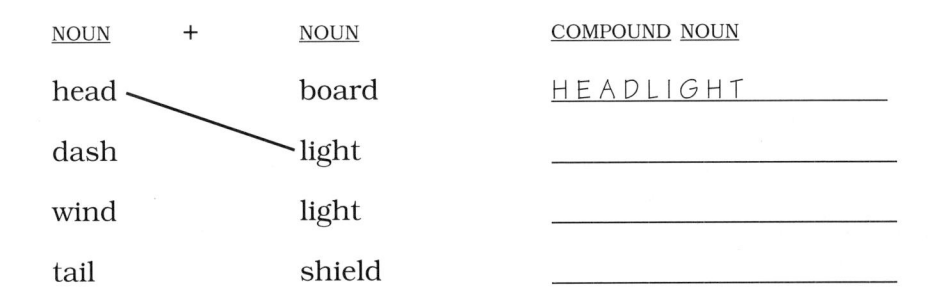

NOUN	+	NOUN	COMPOUND NOUN
head		board	HEADLIGHT
dash		light	_____
wind		light	_____
tail		shield	_____

81

3. There are more than one of these items on a car. Write the plural form.

SINGULAR	PLURAL
1. headlight	two HEADLIGHTS
2. brake	four _____
3. wheel	four _____
4. seat belt	two or more _____
5. seat	two or more _____
6. bumper	two _____
7. windshield wiper	two _____
8. taillight	two _____
9. tire	four _____
10. turn signal	four _____

4. Write the noun form for each of these verbs.

You will add either *-r*, *-er*, or *-or*.

VERB	NOUN	VERB	NOUN
1. drive	DRIVER	4. accelerate	_____
2. bump	_____	5. radiate	_____
3. wipe	_____		

5. Draw a line between words that make a noun phrase. Write the noun phrase.

NOUN	+	NOUN	NOUN PHRASE
spare		mirror	SPARE TIRE
steering		wheel	_____
windshield		seat	_____
passenger		wiper	_____
glove		signal	_____
turn		tire	_____
rearview		belt	_____
gas		plate	_____
license		compartment	_____
seat		tank	_____

6. Where would you most likely store these items? Write the words under the appropriate location.

	GLOVE COMPARTMENT	TRUNK
maps	MAPS	
luggage		
spare tire		
extra change		
jack		
pencil		

READING PRACTICE

1. Which underlined word is incorrect? Circle the letter.

> **GRAMMAR TO KNOW:**
> causative verbs   modal auxiliaries
> prepositions   word families

1. Maria is always <u>carefully</u> not to <u>get</u> a flat tire <u>because</u> she has no spare.
                         Ⓐ   B   C

2. <u>Because</u> <u>the</u> battery was dead, the engine <u>will</u> not start.
      A   B   C

3. This new sedan <u>has</u> <u>a</u> large trunk and a <u>comfortably</u> driver's seat.
                        A B   C

4. I will have Carrie <u>filling</u> up the gas tank <u>so</u> that you can <u>get</u> an early start.
                   A   B   C

5. <u>After</u> the accident, the car's rear bumper <u>and</u> taillights <u>will</u> not work.
     A   B   C

6. <u>I'll</u> have Steven <u>wore</u> his seat belt if he rides in the <u>passenger</u> seat.
    A   B   C

7. If you keep an eye <u>in</u> your speedometer, you will <u>drive</u> at <u>the</u> proper speed.
                   A   B C

8. The speedometer <u>is</u> <u>convenient</u> located <u>on</u> the dashboard of a car.
                   A B   C

9. <u>Be</u> sure to have the brakes, the battery, the engine <u>and</u> the steering
    A   B
   <u>checking</u> before a long trip.
     C

10. If you must drive <u>in</u> a rainy night, <u>check</u> the windshield wipers, the tires
                      A   B
    <u>and</u> the brakes.
     C

2. Read the following conversation and answer the questions.

> Jane: My car isn't old, but there's always something wrong with it.
> Mel: What now? Didn't you just have the brakes fixed?
> Jane: Yes. This time it seems to be the steering wheel. It's hard to turn.
> Mel: That could be dangerous. You'd better take it back to the mechanic.

1. The car is NOT
   (A) old
   (B) fast
   (C) small

2. What was recently repaired on the car?
   (A) The brakes
   (B) The hood
   (C) The wheels

3. What is hard to turn?
   (A) The rearview mirror
   (B) The steering wheel
   (C) The radio dial

4. Jane will probably
   (A) sell the car
   (B) not drive the car again
   (C) take the car to the mechanic

3. Read the following paragraph and answer the questions.

> When you get ready to drive, there are several things to do before you start the car. Check the rearview mirror. Make sure you can see clearly out the back window. Put on your seat belt. Turn on the ignition; make sure that you have enough gas. Always accelerate slowly, and, most importantly, drive cautiously.

1. This passage gives advice on
   (A) starting to drive
   (B) parking a car
   (C) using a gas station

2. The purpose of the rearview mirror is to let you see
   (A) your face clearly
   (B) out the back window
   (C) straight ahead

3. Which of these in NOT mentioned in the passage?
   (A) Put on your seat belt.
   (B) Turn on the radio.
   (C) Accelerate slowly.

4. Which of the following is the MOST important?
   (A) Have a full tank of gas.
   (B) Keep your windows clean.
   (C) Drive cautiously.

22 ROADS

WORDS TO KNOW

beltway	honk	parkway	throughway
bus	lane	pass	toll booth
circle	median	rest stop	trailer
drive	merge	route	truck
exit	motorbike	signal	turnpike
freeway	motorcycle	speed	van
highway	overpass	speed limit	yield

WORD PRACTICE

1. Write the appropriate words for different types of high-speed roads.

1. A road that goes through a park land   P A R K W A Y
2. A road without stop lights   T _ _ _ _ _ _ W _ _
3. A road that goes around a city like a belt   B _ _ _ W _ _
4. A road without intersections   F _ _ _ W _ _
5. A general term for a high-speed road   H _ _ _ W _ _

2. Write the simple verb form of these *-ing* words.

1. merging   MERGE
2. passing
3. driving
4. yielding
5. speeding
6. honking

3. Fill in the blanks.

Passing on a Highway

It is permissible to go faster than the S _ _ _ D limit on a H _ _ _ W _ Y when you P _ _ S another car. Be sure to leave lots of room and to use your turn S _ G _ _ _ .

85

4. Write the words under the appropriate category.

van	overpass	median
highway	truck	bus
trailer	motorcycle	yield
pass	honk	drive
merge	lane	rest stop

VEHICLE	ACTION	LOCATION
VAN	PASS	HIGHWAY
_____	_____	_____
_____	_____	_____
_____	_____	_____
_____	_____	_____

5. Fill in the blanks.

A Toll Road

Sometimes we must pay a T _ _ _ to use some roads. Some toll roads are called T _ _ _ P _ K _ S. We pay the toll to people who sit in toll B _ _ T _ S. Toll booths are located at either the entrances to the turnpikes or the E X _ _ S from the turnpikes.

6. What form of transportation do I need? Write the answer.

1. Forty people want a city tour.

    I need a B U S.

2. I need to deliver quickly a small package during rush hour.

    I need a M _ _ _ _ B _ K _.

3. My family is taking a vacation in the mountains.

    I need a T _ _ _ _ _ _ attached to my car.

4. I am moving my furniture to a new house.

    I need a T _ _ _ _.

5. I am taking my daughter's friends to the tennis match.

    I need a V _ _.

7. Draw a line between the nouns that make compound nouns. Write the compound noun next to it.

NOUN	+	NOUN	COMPOUND NOUN
1. belt		pass	B E L T W A Y
2. motor		pike	_____
3. over		way	_____
4. motor		bike	_____
5. turn		cycle	_____

READING PRACTICE

1. Which underlined word is incorrect? Circle the letter.

> **GRAMMAR TO KNOW:**
> conditional sentences   infinitives
> prepositions   verb tense

1. A <u>fast</u> way <u>getting</u> across town and avoid local traffic <u>is</u> on the freeway.
   A   Ⓑ   C

2. When <u>entering</u> the turnpike, be sure <u>to</u> yield <u>of</u> oncoming traffic.
        A   B   C

3. If you <u>don't</u> want <u>to startle</u> a motorcycle driver, <u>passed</u> him slowly.
       A   B   C

4. There was a circle <u>at</u> the intersection of these two routes, <u>but</u> now there
                         A   B
<u>was</u> an overpass.
 C

5. If you <u>feel</u> tired while <u>driving</u> on the turnpike, <u>pulled</u> into a rest stop.
       A   B   C

6. Trucks and trailers should stay <u>of</u> one side <u>of</u> the tollbooth while cars and
                                      A   B
vans <u>stay</u> on the other.
      C

7. Take the throughway <u>to</u> the beltway and then <u>got</u> off <u>at</u> Exit 7.
                       A   B   C

8. If you are caught <u>speeding</u> <u>on</u> the highway, you will <u>paid</u> a large fine.
                 A   B   C

9. It <u>is</u> extremely dangerous <u>drove</u> over the median <u>of</u> a highway.
   A   B   C

10. When you <u>drive</u> onto the parkway, you must <u>merged</u> <u>with</u> the left lanes.
           A   B   C

2. Read the following conversation and answer the questions.

Driver:	How do I get to the National Park?
Toll booth attendant:	Stay on the turnpike until Exit 15. That's the beltway around Philadelphia. Stay on the beltway until Exit 5A. Keep in the right hand lane because the exit is very close. The park is at the exit.
Driver:	Do I pay the toll now?
Toll booth attendant:	No, pay when you get off the turnpike.
Driver:	What's the speed limit on the turnpike?
Toll booth attendant:	The same as any highway–55 mph.

1. Where is the driver going?
   (A) To Philadelphia
   (B) To the National Park
   (C) To the toll booth

2. What is the driver's first exit?
   (A) Exit 15
   (B) Exit 5A
   (C) Exit 51

3. What highway circles Philadelphia?
   (A) The turnpike
   (B) The beltway
   (C) The parkway

4. What is the speed limit on the turnpike?
   (A) Less than the beltway
   (B) More than the freeway
   (C) The same as any highway

3. Read the following paragraph and answer the questions.

> The highway system makes it possible to cover hundreds of miles in a day. The speed limit is high, and rest stops along the road allow drivers to leave the highway and stop and eat. Once they have rested, drivers can easily and quickly get back on the highway.

1. How many miles can a person drive in one day on a highway?
   (A) Hundreds
   (B) Thousands
   (C) Dozens

2. Where can drivers stop and eat quickly?
   (A) At expensive restaurants
   (B) At rest stops
   (C) At toll booths

3. The speed limit on highways is
   (A) low
   (B) high
   (C) excessive

4. How much time do most drivers spend at a rest stop?
   (A) A short while
   (B) Several days
   (C) One week

23 THE BODY

WORDS TO KNOW

ankle	face	knee	shoulder
arm	finger	leg	stomach
back	fist	lip	thigh
beard	foot	moustache	throat
cheek	forehead	mouth	thumb
chest	hair	muscle	toe
chin	hand	nail	tongue
ear	head	neck	tooth
elbow	heart	nose	waist
eye	hip	palm	wrist

WORD PRACTICE

1. Label these parts of the body.

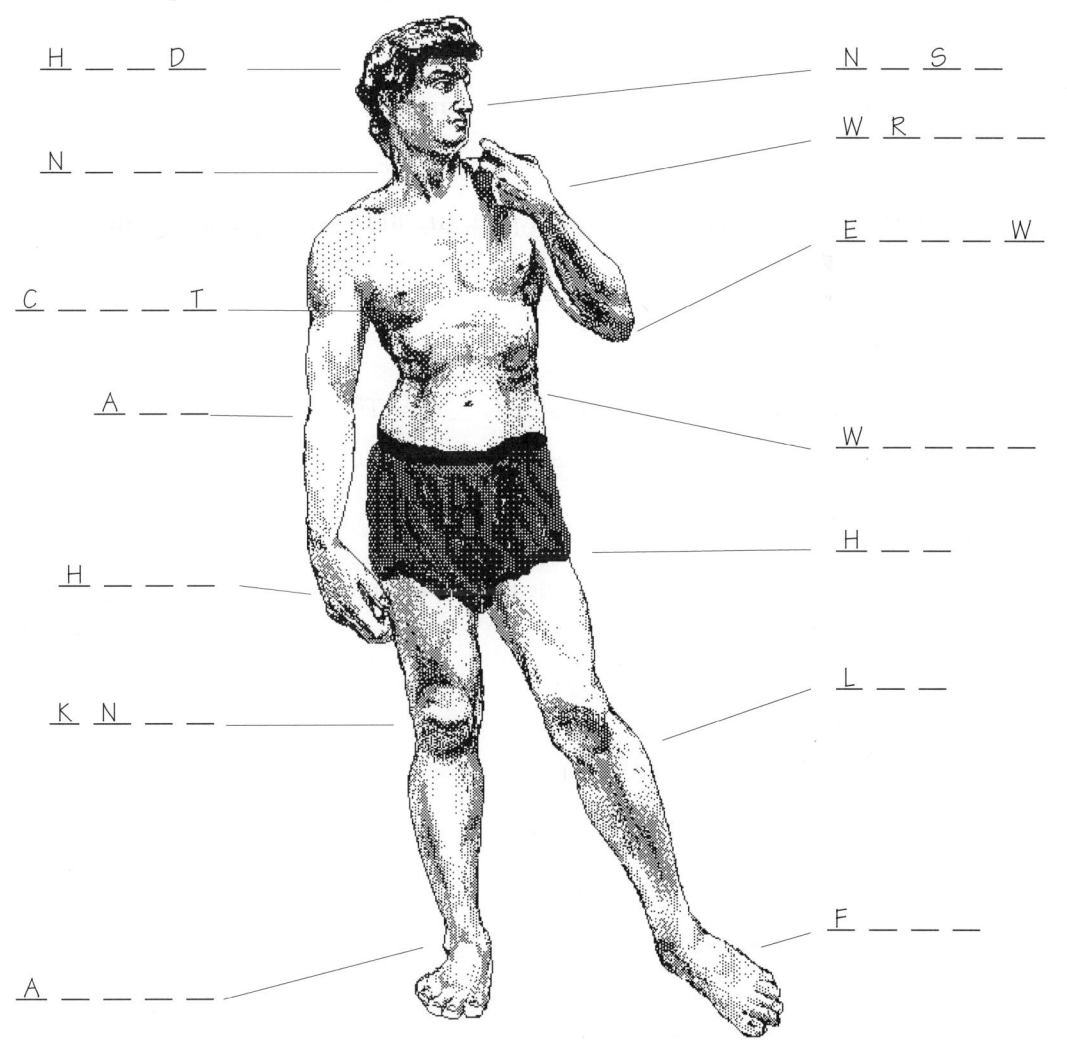

- H _ _ D _ _ _ _
- N _ _ _
- C _ _ _ T
- A _ _
- H _ _ _
- K N _ _ _
- A _ _ _
- N _ S _
- W R _ _ _
- E _ _ W
- W _ _ _ _
- H _ _
- L _ _
- F _ _ _

2. Idiom Practice: Complete the sentences.

1. He's at the H E A D of his class. = *He's the best.*
2. Don't try to E _ _ _ _ your way in. = *Don't push yourself in.*
3. I've got them in the P _ _ _ of my H _ _ _ . = *I'm in control.*
4. He has a L _ _ up on this. = *He has the advantage.*
5. I have two left F _ _ _ . = *I'm very clumsy.*
6. Don't M _ _ _ _ _ in. = *Don't try to be a part of this.*
7. Keep your L _ _ _ sealed. = *Don't talk.*
8. She gave me the cold S _ _ _ _ _ _ _ . = *She ignored me.*
9. I can't S _ _ _ _ _ _ his opinion. = *I don't like his opinion.*
10. He's all T _ _ _ _ _ . = *He's very clumsy.*
11. He has a big M _ _ _ _ . = *He can't keep a secret.*
12. She has a sharp T _ _ _ _ _ . = *She is unkind.*
13. Keep your E _ _ _ peeled. = *Look out for something.*
14. Turn the other C _ _ _ _ . = *Forgive someone.*
15. She is a B _ _ _ _ . = *She's smart.*
16. I know the city like the back of my H _ _ _ . = *I know it very well.*
17. He has a H _ _ _ _ of gold. = *He is kind.*
18. He wears his H _ _ _ _ on his sleeve. = *Everyone knows when he's in love.*
19. This job is a pain in the N _ _ _ . = *This job bothers me.*
20. We don't see E _ _ to E _ _ . = *We don't agree.*
21. I know her from H _ _ _ to T _ _ . = *I know her well.*
22. He turned his B _ _ _ on us. = *He ignored us.*

3. Complete these sentences.

1. Hair covers the top of the H E A D .
2. A moustache is under the N _ _ _ .
3. A beard covers the C _ _ _ .
4. Both toes and fingers have N _ _ L S .
5. The F _ _ _ H _ _ D is between the eyebrows and the hairline.

4. Cross out the word that does NOT belong.

1. lip — mouth — ~~toe~~
2. chin — thigh — beard
3. fist — hand — neck
4. nose — ankle — moustache
5. hip — eye — shoulder
6. thumb — finger — wrist
7. tongue — forehead — tooth
8. stomach — waist — throat
9. ankle — foot — head
10. arm — nail — elbow

READING PRACTICE

1. Which underlined word is incorrect? Circle the letter.

> **GRAMMAR TO KNOW:**
> conditional sentences   articles
> subject-verb agreement   verb tense

1. When Joseph pounded <u>his</u> fist, he <u>hurts</u> <u>his</u> finger.
                             A   (B)   C

2. When I <u>close</u> <u>my</u> eyes, I cannot <u>seen</u>.
              A   B   C

3. The heart <u>is</u> a muscle that <u>pump</u> blood <u>throughout</u> the body.
                A   B   C

4. If you <u>cut</u> your foot, you may <u>found</u> it hard <u>to walk</u>.
         A   B   C

5. Stephanie's forehead <u>and</u> cheeks are so hot she thinks she <u>had</u> <u>a</u> fever.
                            A   B   C

6. When Rocky was <u>punched</u> <u>in</u> <u>a</u> chin, he got a toothache.
                      A   B C

7. <u>My</u> nose and mouth <u>is</u> <u>too</u> large for my face.
     A   B   C

8. If <u>your</u> stomach hurts, <u>maybe</u> it <u>is</u> something you ate.
       A   B   C

9. My father <u>has</u> a thick beard, <u>so</u> you cannot <u>saw</u> his chin.
             A   B   C

10. Pam has <u>a</u> broken wrist so she <u>can't</u> play <u>the</u> tennis for two months.
           A   B   C

2. Read the following conversation and answer the questions.

> Man: My right arm hurts. I wonder if my heart is OK.
> Woman: You should see a doctor, and, in the meantime, rest.
> Man: He's busy until tomorrow.

1. What is the problem?
   (A) The doctor is resting.
   (B) The man is too busy.
   (C) His right arm hurts.

2. What does the woman want the man to do?
   (A) See a doctor
   (B) Get out of bed
   (C) Wait until tomorrow

3. What should he do in the meantime?
   (A) Exercise
   (B) Rest
   (C) Study medicine

4. When is the doctor available?
   (A) Presently
   (B) This evening
   (C) Tomorrow

3. Read the following paragraph and answer the questions.

> Comfortable Clothes
> Shoes must be wide enough for the toes; the pants must be long enough in the legs and wide enough at the waist. The jacket must not be tight across the chest, and the sleeves should not be too short for the arms.

1. Pants must not be too narrow at the
   (A) chest
   (B) waist
   (C) shoulder

2. Shoes must not be too narrow for the
   (A) fingers
   (B) toes
   (C) ears

3. A jacket must fit comfortably across the
   (A) palm
   (B) ankle
   (C) chest

4. Sometimes the sleeves may not fit the
   (A) arms
   (B) legs
   (C) feet

24 CLOTHES

WORDS TO KNOW

alter	glove	raincoat	sock
belt	hat	running shoes	suit
blouse	jacket	scarf	sweater
boots	lapel	shirt	take off
briefcase	overcoat	shoelace	tennis shoes
button	pants	shoes	tie
coat	pocket	skirt	trousers
collar	purse	slacks	try on
cuff	put away	sleeve	T-shirt
dress	put on	sneakers	umbrella

WORD PRACTICE

1. Complete the following sentences.

1. I put on my S O C K S before I put on my shoes.
2. If it is raining, I wear a R _ _ _ C _ _ _ and carry an U _ B _ _ _ _ A.
3. I broke a S _ _ _ _ A _ _ when I was tying my shoes.
4. I use a B _ _ _ to hold up my pants.
5. If the weather is cool, I will wear a S W _ _ _ _ _.
6. The shirt C _ _ _ _ R is too tight around my neck.
7. A B _ _ _ _ N is missing from my shirt cuff.
8. The color of her S K _ _ _ matches the color of her P _ _ S _.
9. It's windy so I'll wear a J _ _ K _ _.
10. The tailor who added C _ _ F _ to my pants charges for alteration.

2. Draw a line between similar items of clothing.

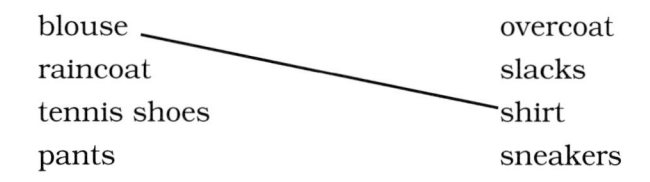

blouse — shirt
raincoat — overcoat
tennis shoes — sneakers
pants — slacks

93

3. Label the clothes.

1. GLASSES
2. _____
3. _____
4. _____
5. _____
6. _____
7. _____
8. _____
9. _____
10. _____

4. Which of the following are referred to "in pairs"? Write them below.

pants	purse	belt	socks
T-shirt	shoes	trousers	boots
slacks	gloves	jacket	hat

1. A pair of ___PANTS___
2. A pair of _____
3. A pair of _____
4. A pair of _____
5. A pair of _____
6. A pair of _____
7. A pair of _____

5. Write the word under the appropriate category.

	WORN ABOVE THE WAIST	WORN BELOW THE WAIST
tie	TIE	
shirt		
boots		
shorts		
running shoes		
shoe laces		
tennis shoes		
T-shirt		
sweater		
jacket		

6. Complete the following sentences.

1. In the morning when I get dressed, I put <u>O N</u> my shirt before I _ _ _ on my pants.

2. In the evening before I go to bed, I take _ _ _ my shoes before I _ _ _ _ off my socks.

3. When my shirts come back from the laundry, I put them <u>A</u> _ _ _ .

7. Fill in the blanks.

1. On my feet I wear <u>S H O E S</u> .

2. On my head, I wear a <u>H</u> _ _ .

3. Around my neck I wear a <u>S</u> _ _ _ _ or a <u>T</u> _ _ .

READING PRACTICE

1. Which underlined word is incorrect? Circle the letter.

> **GRAMMAR TO KNOW:**
> articles			infinitives
> subject-verb agreement	verb tense

1. <u>My</u> new jacket needs <u>being</u> altered <u>because</u> the sleeves are too long.
   A   Ⓑ   C

2. Suzanne <u>always</u> carries a purse <u>but</u> a briefcase when she <u>goes</u> to work.
          A   B   C

3. Will you <u>got</u> my wallet? <u>It's</u> <u>in</u> my pants pocket.
              A   B C

4. When wearing <u>a</u> suit, the right choice <u>of</u> a tie and shoes <u>are</u> essential.
                  A   B   C

5. Scott <u>wear</u> his boots <u>to</u> work every day <u>and</u> puts on his shoes in the office.
          A   B   C

6. I <u>was</u> getting my raincoat <u>and</u> umbrella out <u>of</u> the closet now.
      A   B   C

7. Bob <u>came</u> dressed casually, in tennis shoes, <u>a</u> T-shirt <u>also</u> running shorts.
        A   B   C

8. Will you <u>try on</u> this sweater? It <u>didn't</u> <u>fit</u> me anymore.
              A   B   C

9. These slacks <u>need</u> a belt <u>because</u> they <u>is</u> too big for you.
                  A   B   C

10. If you want <u>wearing</u> one <u>of</u> my skirts, or a blouse, you <u>may</u>.
                  A   B   C

95

2. Read the following conversation and answer the questions.

> Customer: I would like this suit altered, please.
> Tailor: Please try it on for me.
> Customer: I want to have the sleeves shortened, and the lapels made narrower.
> Tailor: What about the pants? Do you want a cuff?
> Customer: No, I prefer pants without a cuff.

1. What does the customer want altered?
   (A) His suit
   (B) His shirt
   (C) His coat

2. What is wrong with the sleeves?
   (A) They're too short.
   (B) They're too long.
   (C) They don't match.

3. What does he want made narrower?
   (A) His sleeves
   (B) His cuffs
   (C) His lapels

4. How does he prefer his pants?
   (A) Tight around the waist
   (B) With a cuff
   (C) Without a cuff

3. Read the following passage and answer the questions.

> I am a very neat person. I keep my bedroom very neat, too. My bedroom closets are very organized. I hang all my shirts together. I hang all my pants together. I hang all my suits together. All of my shoes are arranged in rows on the floor. My ties and belts hang on the closet door. I keep my raincoat and my overcoat in the hall closet downstairs.

1. How would you describe this person?
   (A) Disorganized
   (B) Neat
   (C) Polite

2. Where does he put his shirts?
   (A) In the closet
   (B) In drawers
   (C) Across a chair

3. What does he hang on the closet door?
   (A) His pants
   (B) His suits
   (C) His ties

4. What does he keep in the hall closet?
   (A) His raincoat
   (B) His suits
   (C) His shirts

25 HOUSEWORK

WORDS TO KNOW

ammonia	cord	make the bed	sponge
bleach	detergent	mop	sweep
broom	dust	polish	wash
bucket	dustpan	rug shampoo	washing machine
clean	iron	scrub	water
cleanser	ironing board	soap	vacuum cleaner

WORD PRACTICE

1. Add *-ing* to the following verbs.

1. sweep   _SWEEPING_
2. dust   _____
3. wash   _____
4. clean   _____
5. polish   _____
6. iron   _____

Note these differences:

| mop | mopping |
| scrub | scrubbing |

2. Use the *-ing* words from Exercise 1 to complete these sentences.

1. The woman is S W E E P I N G with a broom.
2. Many people do spring C _ _ _ _ _ _ _ .
3. We use a W _ _ _ _ _ machine to wash clothes.
4. She is D _ _ _ _ _ _ tables with a rag.
5. P _ _ _ _ _ _ _ _ wood makes it shine.
6. To press clothes, an I _ _ _ _ _ _ board is necessary.
7. S C _ _ _ _ _ _ _ will remove heavy dirt.
8. You need to have a bucket full of soap and water and a mop when

    M _ _ _ _ _ _ floors.

97

3. Draw a line between the words that are similar in meaning.

broom — mop
sponge — rag
soap — cleanser
wash — clean
sweep — vacuum

4. Cross out the words that do NOT belong.

1. soap   ~~iron~~   water
2. bucket   cleanser   cord
3. sweep   detergent   washing machine
4. mop   sponge   shower
5. polish   yard   floor

5. Write types of cleaning products.

1. W A T E R
2. C _ _ _ _ S _ R
3. R _ G   S _ _ _ _ _ O
4. P _ _ _ _ H
5. D _ _ _ R _ _ _ T
6. A M _ _ _ _ A
7. B _ _ _ _ H
8. S _ _ P

6. Write the appropriate cleaning product below.

1. I add A M M O N I A to water when I clean the windows.
2. B _ _ _ _ H keeps white clothes looking white.
3. Ajax is a C _ _ _ _ S _ R that cleans sinks.
4. Put D _ _ _ _ _ _ _ T in the washing machine with the clothes.
5. Use very little wax P _ _ _ _ H on wood furniture.
6. There is a bar of S _ _ P next to the bathtub.
7. Plain W _ _ _ R is usually enough to clean.
8. Using a R _ _   S H _ _ _ _ _ will keep your rug clean.

CLEANING EXPRESSIONS

1. Spring cleaning =
   A thorough cleaning

2. Dishpan hands =
   Hands rough from doing dishes

3. Use a bit of elbow grease. =
   Work harder/ rub harder.

4. Sweep the dirt under the rug. =
   Hide a problem.

5. This place is a pig pen. =
   It's really dirty.

READING PRACTICE

1. Which underlined word is incorrect? Circle the letter.

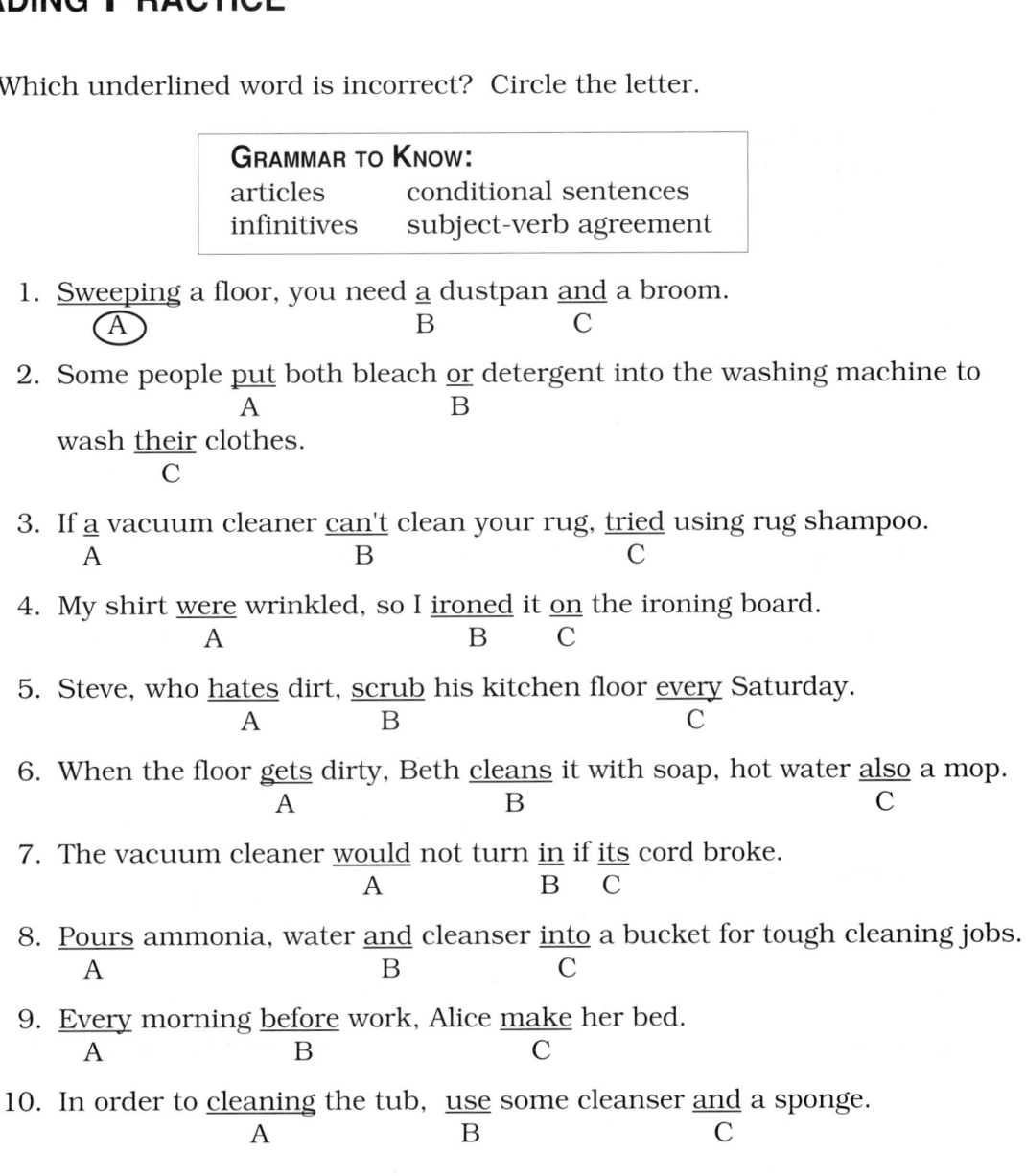

> **GRAMMAR TO KNOW:**
> articles   conditional sentences
> infinitives   subject-verb agreement

1. <u>Sweeping</u> a floor, you need <u>a</u> dustpan <u>and</u> a broom.
   (A)   B   C

2. Some people <u>put</u> both bleach <u>or</u> detergent into the washing machine to
                  A   B
   wash <u>their</u> clothes.
          C

3. If <u>a</u> vacuum cleaner <u>can't</u> clean your rug, <u>tried</u> using rug shampoo.
       A   B   C

4. My shirt <u>were</u> wrinkled, so I <u>ironed</u> it <u>on</u> the ironing board.
              A   B   C

5. Steve, who <u>hates</u> dirt, <u>scrub</u> his kitchen floor <u>every</u> Saturday.
                A   B   C

6. When the floor <u>gets</u> dirty, Beth <u>cleans</u> it with soap, hot water <u>also</u> a mop.
                    A   B   C

7. The vacuum cleaner <u>would</u> not turn <u>in</u> if <u>its</u> cord broke.
                        A   B   C

8. <u>Pours</u> ammonia, water <u>and</u> cleanser <u>into</u> a bucket for tough cleaning jobs.
     A   B   C

9. <u>Every</u> morning <u>before</u> work, Alice <u>make</u> her bed.
     A   B   C

10. In order to <u>cleaning</u> the tub, <u>use</u> some cleanser <u>and</u> a sponge.
                  A   B   C

2. Read the following conversation and answer the questions.

> Mother: Here are today's chores: First, vacuum the rug. Sweep the steps. Wash the windows.
> Child: How do I sweep the steps?
> Mother: With the broom, of course. And wash them after you sweep them.
> Child: Where are the bucket and mop?
> Mother: In the closet. The sponges and ammonia are in there, too.
> Child: Ammonia? What for?
> Mother: For the windows. And don't forget to make your bed and wash the breakfast dishes.
> Child: What about washing the clothes?
> Mother: Good idea. Don't use too much bleach.

1. What does the mother want done first?
   (A) Vacuum the rug
   (B) Sweep the steps
   (C) Wash the windows

2. What will the child use to sweep the steps?
   (A) A broom
   (B) The vacuum
   (C) The mop

3. What is NOT in the closet?
   (A) Sponges
   (B) Ammonia
   (C) Dishes

4. What is the ammonia for?
   (A) Cleaning windows
   (B) Washing clothes
   (C) Drying clothes

3. Read the following paragraph and answer the questions.

> Today many married people share housework equally. A wife may cook, and a husband may clean the house. A wife may wash windows while a husband may scrub the floors. When a husband and wife each have jobs, housework is the responsibility of both.

1. People who share housework are often
   (A) married
   (B) single
   (C) separated

2. Sometimes a woman cooks while her husband
   (A) paints
   (B) travels
   (C) cleans

3. Why do husbands and wives both do housework?
   (A) Both are divorced
   (B) Both have jobs
   (C) Both need money

4. Housework is a
   (A) hobby
   (B) responsibility
   (C) challenge

26 THE LIVING ROOM

WORDS TO KNOW

armchair	couch	lamp	shelf
ashtray	curtains	lamp shade	shelves
bookcase	cushion	mantel	sofa
carpet	drapes	mirror	stereo (set)
ceiling	end table	painting	television
chair	fireplace	picture	wall
coffee table	floor	rug	woodwork

WORD PRACTICE

1. Write the words below for things found on the wall.

1. M I R R O R
2. W _ _ D _ _ _ K
3. M _ _ _ _ L
4. P _ _ _ _ _ E
5. S _ _ _ _ _ S
6. P _ _ _ _ _ _ G

2. The words for some things are often written in plural form. Write them here.

	SINGULAR	PLURAL
1.	curtain	CURTAINS
2.	shelf	_____
3.	end table	_____
4.	drape	_____
5.	picture	_____
6.	chair	_____

101

3. Write the appropriate preposition for each of the following sentences.

CHOICES: in, on, to, above, under

1. The cushions are _____ON_____ the sofa.
2. The books are kept _____ the bookcase.
3. The end tables are next _____ the sofa.
4. The mantle is _____ the fireplace.
5. The carpet is _____ the furniture.
6. The carpet is _____ the floor.

4. Fill in the blanks.

The Fireplace

Many living rooms have a F I R E P L A C E . Above the fireplace is the M _ _ _ _ L , which is a kind of S _ _ _ F used to display special things. Above that is a space where there is often a large M _ _ _ _ R , or a special P _ _ _ _ _ _ _ G .

5. Look at the floor plan. Circle the correct preposition.

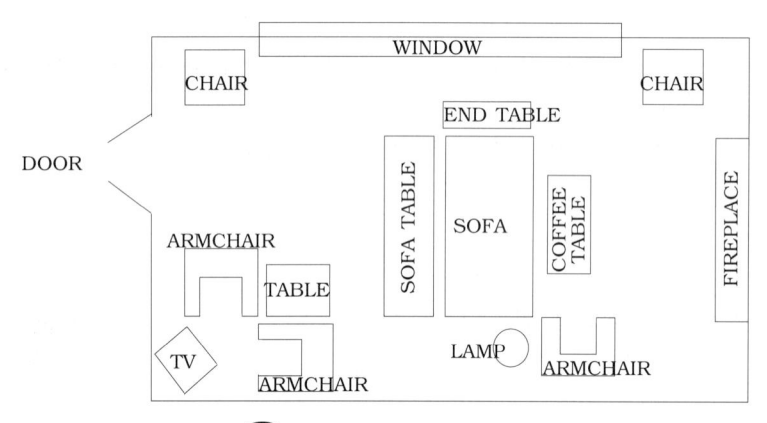

1. There is a chair ((on) / in) either side of the window.
2. There are chairs on both sides (of / to) the window.
3. The coffee table is (in front of / to the side of) the sofa.
4. The sofa table is (behind / over) the sofa.
5. The fireplace is (across from / next to) the door.
6. The TV is (at / in) the corner.
7. There is a small table (between / in front of) the armchairs.
8. There is a lamp (beside / behind) the armchair by the sofa.
9. The end table is (next to / in front of) the sofa.
10. The sofa is (around the corner from / in front of) the fireplace.

6. Draw a line between the nouns that make noun phrases. Write the noun phrase next to it.

NOUN	+	NOUN	NOUN PHRASE
1. lamp		tray	LAMP SHADE
2. wood		chair	_____
3. ash		shade	_____
4. arm		case	_____
5. book		place	_____
6. fire		work	_____

READING PRACTICE

1. Which underlined word is incorrect? Circle the letter.

> **GRAMMAR TO KNOW:**
> conjunctions   prepositions
> subject-verb agreement   verb tense

1. Every night, Stanley sits <u>above</u> the armchair <u>and</u> <u>watches</u> television.
   (A)   B   C

2. The painting <u>on</u> the wall next <u>to</u> the bookcase <u>are</u> of our Aunt Martha.
                  A   B   C

3. The soda fell <u>off</u> the coffee table <u>but</u> <u>onto</u> the carpet.
                  A   B   C

4. The lamp <u>on</u> the end table <u>have</u> <u>a</u> beige lamp shade.
              A   B   C

5. If the contractor builds a low mantel <u>of</u> our fireplace, we can <u>put</u> a large
                                          A   B
   mirror <u>above</u> it.
           C

6. The curtains <u>but</u> the cushions <u>on</u> the sofa are <u>made</u> of the same fabric.
                 A   B   C

7. The woodwork <u>in</u> the <u>Edwards'</u> living room <u>match</u> the mantel.
                 A   B   C

8. <u>Below</u> Emily's stereo <u>is</u> three shelves <u>of</u> records.
    A   B   C

9. The ceiling <u>in</u> our living room <u>is</u> very high, so the room <u>appeared</u> large.
                A   B   C

10. The drapes <u>on</u> our living room windows are thick, <u>allowed</u> very little
                A   B
    light to come <u>into</u> the room.
                   C

103

2. Read the following conversation and answer the questions.

> Byron: Do you want the mirror over the sofa or by the door?
> Melinda: Over the sofa is fine. What about the end table?
> Byron: Let's put it by the armchair.
> Melinda: That's perfect. The painting can go over the bookcase.
> Byron: And we can put the coffee table in front of the sofa. There! Finished!.

1. Where does Melinda want the mirror to go?
   (A) Over the sofa
   (B) Outside
   (C) By the door

2. What are Byron and Melinda doing?
   (A) Sitting on the sofa
   (B) Arranging furniture
   (C) Selling antiques

3. Where will the painting be hung?
   (A) Above the sofa
   (B) Between the windows
   (C) Over the bookcase

4. Where will the coffee table go?
   (A) Next to the armchair
   (B) By the end table
   (C) In front of the sofa

3. Read the following paragraph and answer the questions.

> Living Rooms
>
> Many families use their living rooms as a place for relaxation. It is a place to converse, watch TV, or play music on the stereo. Other families use their living rooms as a more formal place with elegant furniture. They keep the TV and stereo in a family room. They use the living room only when company comes to visit.

1. For many families the living room is a place for
   (A) exercising
   (B) relaxing
   (C) eating

2. Elegant furniture makes a living room
   (A) playful
   (B) rustic
   (C) formal

3. What would NOT fit in a formal living room?
   (A) A TV
   (B) Elegant furniture
   (C) Oil paintings

4. Formal living rooms are used primarily when
   (A) the dining room is too small
   (B) the stereo is broken
   (C) there is company

27 THE KITCHEN

WORDS TO KNOW

bottle	counter	knife	salt shaker
bowl	cup	napkin	saucer
broiler	cutlery	oven	sink
burner	dish	pan	spoon
cabinet	dishwasher	pepper shaker	stove
can	fork	placemat	table
chair	garbage can	plate	tablecloth
coffee maker	garbage disposal	pot	toaster
cook	glass	refrigerator	trash can

WORD PRACTICE

1. Write in the words for electrical appliances.

  1. D I S H W A S H E R
  2. T _ _ _ T _ R
  3. R _ _ _ _ _ _ _ _ T _ R
  4. C _ _ _ _ E _ _ _ _ R
  5. G _ _ _ _ _ _ D _ _ _ _ _ _ L .

2. Circle the words for items found on a table. (6 words)

  oven   spoon   cup
  (plate)   cabinet   cook
  glass   salt shaker   napkin

3. Circle the correct word.

  1. We can cook food in a ((pan) / dishwasher).
  2. A (saucer / trash can) goes under a cup.
  3. You can wash dishes in the (spoon / sink).
  4. Most people use a (can / cabinet) to store dishes.
  5. A (toaster / tablecloth) helps keep a table clean.
  6. We throw (garbage / salt) away.
  7. Put the cutlery on the (placemat / burner).
  8. The cook mixed the ingredients in the (bowl / toaster).
  9. Put the meat under the (broiler / oven) to cook.
  10. Use one (cup / spoon) of water to make one cup of coffee.

4. Write the singular form.

SINGULAR	PLURAL	SINGULAR	PLURAL
1. TABLECLOTH	tablecloths	6. _____	dishes
2. _____	knives	7. _____	bottles
3. _____	glasses	8. _____	cabinets
4. _____	stoves	9. _____	placemats
5. _____	salt shakers	10. _____	napkins

5. Cross out the word that does NOT belong.

1. ~~road~~   tablecloth   placemat
2. plant   fork   knife
3. bottle   can   lamp
4. table   counter   ceiling
5. seat   glass   cup
6. stove   window   refrigerator

6. Write the word that completes the pair.

1. Cup and S A U C E R
2. Knife and F _ _ _
3. Pots and P _ _ S
4. Salt and P _ _ _ _ R

7. Complete the question.

1. What is C U T L E R Y ?

   Knives, forks and spoons.

2. What is a C _ _ _ _ _ M _ _ _ _ ?

   An appliance that brews coffee.

3. What is a G _ _ _ _ _ _ D _ _ _ _ _ _ _ L ?

   An appliance that grinds garbage.

4. What is an O _ _ _ ?

   A place where meat is roasted or bread is baked.

5. What is a T _ _ _ _ _ R ?

   An appliance that browns bread.

Reading Practice

1. Which underlined word is incorrect? Circle the letter.

> **GRAMMAR TO KNOW:**
> conjunctions   pronouns
> subject-verb agreement   articles

1. <u>Setting</u> the table, we'll <u>need</u> plates, knives, forks, placemats <u>and</u> glasses.
   (A)   B   C

2. Kevin <u>keeps</u> his pots <u>but</u> pans in the cabinet <u>below</u> the stove.
   A   B   C

3. We don't <u>has</u> a garbage disposal so we <u>throw</u> garbage <u>in</u> the garbage can.
   A   B   C

4. Little Amy's baby bottle and <u>she</u> dish <u>are</u> in <u>the</u> dishwasher.
   A   B   C

5. Will you please <u>pass</u> me the salt shaker <u>and</u> the bowl of <u>the</u> spaghetti?
   A   B   C

6. Angela's counter <u>have</u> many appliances <u>on</u> it: the coffee maker, the
   A   B

   toaster, <u>and</u> the can opener.
            C

7. <u>Our</u> want coffee so we'll <u>need</u> cups, saucers, <u>and</u> spoons.
   A   B   C

8. If you want to cook <u>the</u> dinner <u>in</u> the oven, turn <u>them</u> to 350 degrees.
                        A   B   C

9. The food <u>from</u> last night's dinner that <u>were</u> not eaten <u>is</u> in the refrigerator.
              A   B   C

10. Do you want <u>to cook</u> the hamburgers <u>in</u> the broiler <u>and</u> on the stove?
                 A   B   C

EVERYDAY EXPRESSIONS WITH COOKING TERMS

1. Cooking with gas =
   Thinking/acting efficiently
2. Cooking on all four burners =
   To be very alert and active
3. Don't cry over spilled milk. =
   Don't have regrets.
4. Half-baked idea =
   Not a well thought-out plan
5. Look at the pot calling the kettle black. =
   The accuser is also guilty.
6. The kitchen cabinet =
   A small group of close friends and advisers

2. Read the following conversation and answer the questions.

> Bill: Shall I set the table?
> Susan: Yes. Use the placemats, not a tablecloth.
> Bill: Do you want paper or cloth napkins?
> Susan: Paper. And we won't need plates. This soup will be the whole meal. We'll only need bowls.
> Bill: OK. No forks or knives either. Just spoons, right?

1. What is Bill going to do?
   (A) Buy napkins
   (B) Make soup
   (C) Set the table

2. What will they use on the table?
   (A) A tablecloth
   (B) Placemats
   (C) Furniture polish

3. What kind of napkins will they use?
   (A) Paper
   (B) Cloth
   (C) Plastic

4. What cutlery will they use?
   (A) Knives
   (B) Forks
   (C) Spoons

3. Read the following paragraph and answer the questions.

> Modern kitchens are different from older kitchens in several ways. There are more appliances, of course. Usually the modern kitchen is larger. There is more counter space for food preparation. Modern kitchens are also full of light. There are many more windows than in older kitchens.

1. This paragraph compares modern and older
   (A) windows
   (B) counters
   (C) kitchens

2. Modern kitchens are not
   (A) different
   (B) dark
   (C) large

3. In a modern kitchen there is more space to prepare
   (A) light
   (B) food
   (C) appliances

4. Why does the modern kitchen have more light?
   (A) Brighter bulbs
   (B) More lamps
   (C) More windows

28 THE POST OFFICE

WORDS TO KNOW

address	letter	postal clerk	sort
air	mailbox	postal code	special delivery
counter	mail carrier	postcard	stamp
deliver	overnight mail	postmark	surface
envelope	package	post office box	weigh
first class	parcel post	return address	window
label	postage	seal	zip code

WORD PRACTICE

1. Complete these sentences.

1. The mail is delivered by the P O S T   O F F I C E.
2. This L _ _ _ _ R weighs 2 ounces.
3. A postcard needs a 25-cent S T _ _ _.
4. The postal C _ _ _ K stands behind a C _ _ _ T E R in the post office.
5. The P _ _ _ M _ _ _ on this letter was July 15.
6. Send this package by P _ R _ _ _ post.
7. P.O.B. stands for post O _ _ _ _ _ B _ _.
8. In the United States, a postal code is called a Z _ _ C _ _ _.
9. The mailing L _ _ _ _ tells the post office where to deliver the package.
10. A F _ _ _ _ C L _ _ _ stamp costs more than a fourth class one.

2. Write six words or phrases that have "*post*" as part of the word or phrase.

1. POSTAGE
2. _____
3. _____
4. _____
5. _____
6. _____

109

3. Write these sentences in the correct order. What happens first?

I read the letter.
I seal and stamp my letter.
I open the envelope.
I look in my mail box.

I write a reply.
I see my mail.
I put my reply into an envelope.
I take it to the post office.

1. I LOOK IN MY MAILBOX.
2. _____
3. _____
4. _____
5. _____
6. _____
7. _____
8. _____

4. Complete the sentences.

1. PROBLEM: The package must arrive tomorrow.
   SOLUTION: Send it O V E R N I G H T mail.

2. PROBLEM: I don't know how much postage is required.
   SOLUTION: The postal clerk will W _ _ _ _ the letter.

3. PROBLEM: My mail doesn't arrive at my home.
   SOLUTION: Use a P _ _ _ O F _ _ _ _ box.

4. PROBLEM: This package is too heavy to send by air.
   SOLUTION: Send it S _ _ _ _ _ E mail.

5. PROBLEM: I don't know when this letter was sent.
   SOLUTION: Look at the P _ _ _ M _ _ K on the envelope.

110

5. Label the parts of the envelope.

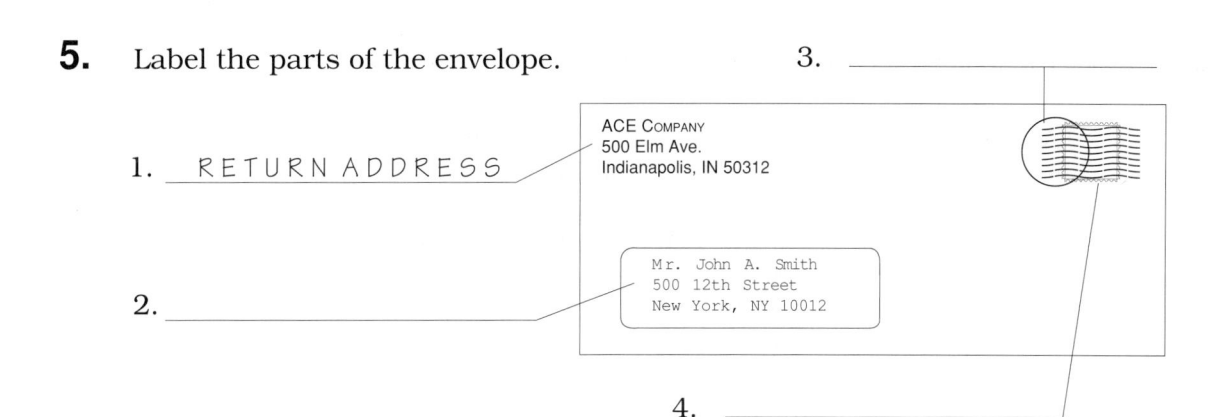

1. _RETURN ADDRESS_

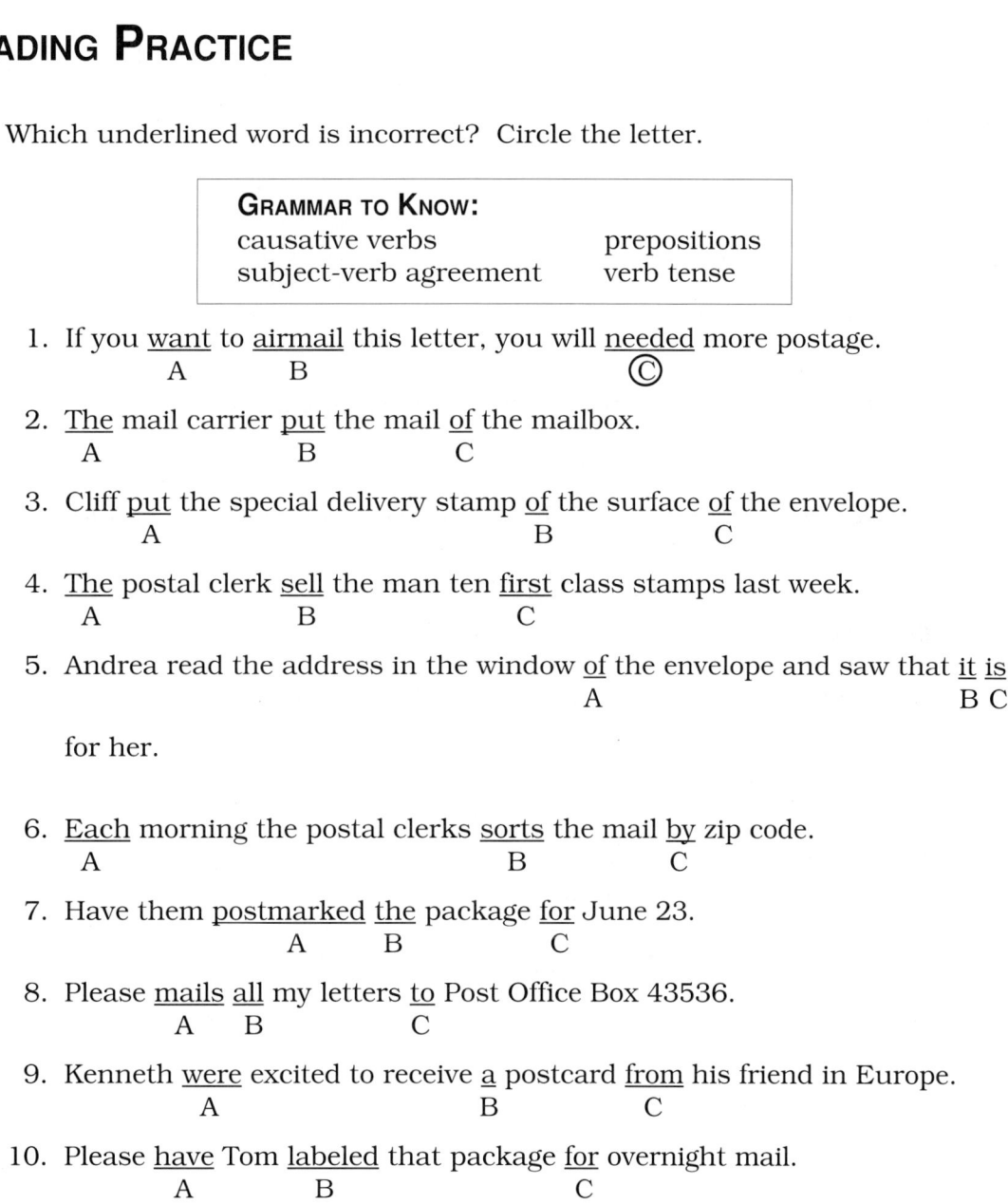

2. _____

3. _____

4. _____

```
ACE COMPANY
500 Elm Ave.
Indianapolis, IN 50312

            Mr. John A. Smith
            500 12th Street
            New York, NY 10012
```

READING PRACTICE

1. Which underlined word is incorrect? Circle the letter.

> **GRAMMAR TO KNOW:**
> causative verbs   prepositions
> subject-verb agreement   verb tense

1. If you <u>want</u> to <u>airmail</u> this letter, you will <u>needed</u> more postage.
       A   B   Ⓒ

2. <u>The</u> mail carrier <u>put</u> the mail <u>of</u> the mailbox.
     A   B   C

3. Cliff <u>put</u> the special delivery stamp <u>of</u> the surface <u>of</u> the envelope.
        A   B   C

4. <u>The</u> postal clerk <u>sell</u> the man ten <u>first</u> class stamps last week.
     A   B   C

5. Andrea read the address in the window <u>of</u> the envelope and saw that <u>it</u> <u>is</u>
                                           A   B C

   for her.

6. <u>Each</u> morning the postal clerks <u>sorts</u> the mail <u>by</u> zip code.
     A   B   C

7. Have them <u>postmarked</u> <u>the</u> package <u>for</u> June 23.
            A   B   C

8. Please <u>mails</u> <u>all</u> my letters <u>to</u> Post Office Box 43536.
      A   B   C

9. Kenneth <u>were</u> excited to receive <u>a</u> postcard <u>from</u> his friend in Europe.
        A   B   C

10. Please <u>have</u> Tom <u>labeled</u> that package <u>for</u> overnight mail.
        A   B   C

2. Read the following conversation and answer the questions.

Customer:	I'd like to mail this package to Hong Kong.
Postal Clerk:	How would you like to send it? By air or surface?
Customer:	By air. A boat would take too long.
Postal Clerk:	It's very heavy. Why don't you send it parcel post by air? It will take 2 weeks and be less expensive.
Customer:	No, I want to send it overnight. It must be there tomorrow.

1. What is the customer doing?
   (A) Mailing a letter
   (B) Taking a boat
   (C) Sending a package

2. What is wrong with surface mail?
   (A) It's too expensive.
   (B) It's too slow.
   (C) It's unreasonable.

3. What service does the clerk recommend?
   (A) Parcel post by air
   (B) Special delivery
   (C) First class

4. When should the package arrive?
   (A) This afternoon
   (B) Tomorrow
   (C) After 2 weeks

3. Read the following announcement and answer the questions.

> ADVICE FROM YOUR POST OFFICE:
> When addressing an envelope, it is important to write clearly. Addresses are often read by machine and sorted by zip code. You must have the correct postage and your return address on every envelope.

1. When is it important to write clearly?
   (A) When writing your mother
   (B) When taking a test
   (C) When addressing an envelope

2. How are envelopes sorted?
   (A) By zip code
   (B) By return address
   (C) By date

3. How much postage is required?
   (A) None if mailed early
   (B) Double the required amount
   (C) The correct amount

4. What is required on every envelope?
   (A) Insufficient postage
   (B) A return address
   (C) Today's postmark

29 FOOD

WORDS TO KNOW

apples	cookies	meat	rice
bacon	corn	milk	rotten
beans	crackers	oil	salad
bread	cream	old	salt
butter	eggs	onions	sandwich
cake	fish	oranges	stale
carrots	flour	peaches	stew
cereal	fresh	pears	sugar
cheese	grapes	pepper	tea
chicken	ice cream	pie	tomatoes
coffee	lettuce	potatoes	vinegar

WORD PRACTICE

1. Write the following kinds of foods.

DAIRY GOODS

1. B U T T E R
2. E _ _ S
3. C _ _ _ _ E
4. M _ _ K
5. C _ _ _ M

BAKED GOODS

1. C R _ _ _ _ _ S
2. C _ _ E
3. C O _ _ _ _ S
4. B _ _ _ D
5. P _ _

2. Cross out the word that does NOT belong.

1. eggs ~~plant~~ meat
2. cake pie fish
3. fresh milk stale
4. cook drive serve [eat]
5. animal pear apple

3. Draw a line between food products that are often used together.

eggs   butter
bread   vinegar
coffee   cake
salt   lettuce
ice cream   bacon
tomatoes   pepper
oil   cream

113

4. The words for some food products are usually used in the singular form. Write them here.

1. S A L T
2. F _ _ H
3. C _ _ N
4. R _ _ E
5. L _ _ _ _ _ E

6. S _ _ _ R
7. C H _ _ _ E
8. B _ _ _ N
9. M _ _ K
10. P _ _ _ _ R

5. The words for some food products are often used in the plural form. Write them here.

SINGULAR	PLURAL	SINGULAR	PLURAL
1. egg	EGGS	4. bean	_____
2. potato	_____	5. onion	_____
3. grape	_____	6. cookie	_____

6. Write the ingredients to make the following dishes.

1. Make a cake

    B U T T E R
    E _ _ S
    F L _ _ _
    M _ _ K
    S _ _ _ _

2. Make a salad

    L _ _ _ _ _ E
    O _ _
    V _ _ _ _ _ _
    T _ _ _ _ _ _ _

3. Make a chicken sandwich

    B R _ _ _
    B _ _ _ _ R
    L _ _ T _ _ _ _
    C H _ _ _ _ _ _
    T _ _ _ _ _ _ _

4. Make a stew

    M _ _ T
    S _ _ T
    P _ _ P _ _
    C _ _ _ _ _ _
    O N _ _ _ _

114

Reading Practice

1. Which underlined word is incorrect? Circle the letter.

> **GRAMMAR TO KNOW:**
> conditional sentences   prepositions
> subject-verb agreement   verb tense

1. <u>When</u> we returned from vacation, we <u>find</u> stale bread <u>and</u> rotten, old
     A   (B)   C

   lettuce in the refrigerator.

2. Mom's apple pie <u>are</u> the perfect afternoon <u>snack</u> or <u>dessert</u>.
                     A   B   C

3. Every Sunday, the Petersons <u>eat</u> bacon <u>and</u> eggs <u>of</u> breakfast.
                                    A   B   C

4. If you are hungry, <u>ate</u> some <u>of</u> the pears, oranges and grapes <u>in</u>
                          A   B   C

   the fruit bowl.

5. Last night we <u>ate</u> fresh fish with corn <u>and</u> rice <u>in</u> dinner.
                   A   B   C

6. My favorite recipe <u>are</u> the one <u>with</u> chicken, beans, <u>and</u> cheese.
                        A   B   C

7. If you <u>would</u> like a cup of coffee, <u>took</u> some cream <u>and</u> sugar.
            A   B   C

8. I <u>making</u> simple salads <u>with</u> lettuce, tomatoes, oil <u>and</u> vinegar.
      A   B   C

9. <u>Stop</u> snacking on cookies <u>and</u> crackers. Dinner will be <u>at</u> one hour.
    A   B   C

10. David always <u>puts</u> salt <u>and</u> pepper <u>at</u> his meat before eating it.
                     A   B   C

> **FOOD EXPRESSIONS**
>
> 1. Food for thought = Something to think about
>
> 2. She's the apple of his eye. = She is very fond of him.
>
> 3. Bring home the bacon. = Earn a living.
>
> 4. He's no spring chicken. = He's not very young.

2. Read the following conversation and answer the questions.

> John: Are these eggs fresh?
> Bill: No, I bought them last week. The bread is a week old, too.
> John: No wonder it's stale.
> Bill: And this milk tastes sour.
> John: That milk is two weeks old. Like the lettuce.
> Bill: Everything in this refrigerator is rotten.

1. What does NOT describe the eggs?
   (A) Fresh
   (B) Sweet
   (C) Expensive

2. What is stale?
   (A) The eggs
   (B) The milk
   (C) The bread

3. How does the milk taste?
   (A) Sweet
   (B) Sour
   (C) Creamy

4. What describes the food in the refrigerator?
   (A) Rotten
   (B) Fresh
   (C) Tasty

3. Read the following paragraph and answer the questions.

> The supermarket has special sections for different kinds of foods. Milk, cream, and cheese are kept in the Dairy Section. Chicken, fish, and meat are kept in the Meat Section. Canned fruits and vegetables are kept on shelves. Fresh fruits and vegetables are kept in the Produce Section. Baked goods like bread, pies, cakes, and cookies also have their own sections.

1. Where is cream kept?
   (A) With the coffee
   (B) In the Diary Section
   (C) With the canned goods

2. What is NOT in the Meat Section?
   (A) Chicken
   (B) Fish
   (C) Fruits

3. Where are fresh vegetables found?
   (A) In the Produce Section
   (B) In the Bakery Section
   (C) On the canned goods shelves

4. What are breads, pies, and cakes?
   (A) Canned goods
   (B) Baked goods
   (C) Produce

30 MONEY

WORDS TO KNOW

bank	charge	money	quarter
billfold	check	nickel	receipt
bills	coin	pay	save
budget	credit card	payment	small change
cash	dime	penny	spend
cent	dollar	piggybank	tax
change	earn	purse	wallet

WORD PRACTICE

1. Draw a line between words with similar meanings.

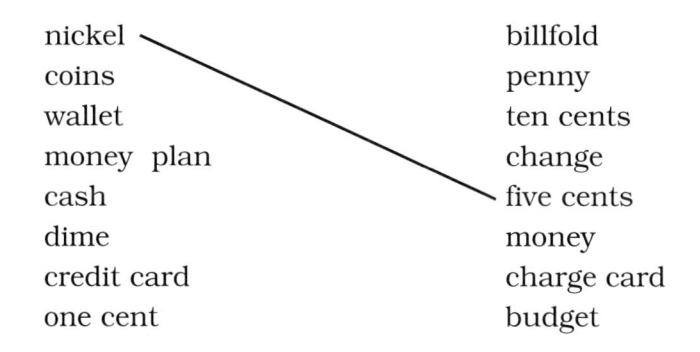

nickel — billfold
coins — penny
wallet — ten cents
money plan — change
cash — five cents
dime — money
credit card — charge card
one cent — budget

2. Write the Present Tense form (1st person singular) for the Past Tense verbs.

PRESENT	PAST
1. SPEND	spent
2. _____	charged
3. _____	paid
4. _____	earned
5. _____	saved

3. Cross out the word that does NOT belong.

1. dime — ~~bank~~ — nickel — penny
2. purse — wallet — billfold — tax
3. forget — spend — save — earn
4. cash — credit card — check — meal
5. coins — bills — pen — money

117

4. Supply the words for types of coins.

1. A <u>Q U A R T E R</u> and a <u>D</u> _ _ _ = 35 cents.
2. Two <u>D</u> _ _ _ <u>S</u> and a <u>N</u> _ _ _ _ _ = 25 cents.
3. Two <u>Q</u> _ _ _ _ _ _ <u>S</u> = 50 cents.
4. Three <u>N</u> _ _ _ _ _ _ and five <u>D</u> _ _ _ <u>S</u> = 65 cents.
5. Three <u>Q</u> _ _ _ _ _ _ _ and twenty-five <u>P</u> _ _ _ _ _ _ = one _ _ _ _ _ _ .

5. Complete the following sentences.

1. It is necessary to have <u>C O I N S</u> for a parking meter.
2. People usually write a <u>C</u> _ _ _ _ for large purchases.
3. Always get a <u>R</u> _ _ _ _ _ _ as proof of purchase.
4. Children often save their pennies in a <u>P</u> _ _ _ _ _ _ _ _ <u>K</u>
5. Most people pay <u>T</u> _ _ _ <u>S</u> to the government.
6. You can pay for something later with a <u>C</u> _ _ _ _ _ _ <u>C</u> _ _ _ .

6. Complete the questions.

1. What is a <u>R E C E I P T</u>?

   A piece of paper with the cost of an item and its purchase date.

2. What is a <u>C</u> _ _ _ _ _ _ <u>C</u> _ _ _ _ ?

   A small plastic card used instead of checks or money.

3. What is a <u>B</u> _ _ _ _ _ _ <u>L</u> _ ?

   A pocket size case for carrying paper money.

4. What is a <u>P</u> _ _ _ _ _ _ _ ?

   The amount of money paid or to be paid.

5. What is a <u>B</u> _ _ _ _ _ _ ?

   An itemized summary of future income and expenses.

READING PRACTICE

1. Which underlined word is incorrect? Circle the letter.

> **GRAMMAR TO KNOW:**
> modal auxiliaries   articles
> subject-verb agreement   prepositions

1. Jason always <u>keep</u> all his bills neatly <u>tucked</u> into <u>a</u> billfold.
   Ⓐ   B   C

2. I <u>will</u> like to save <u>some</u> money to pay my <u>own</u> college tuition.
   A   B   C

3. I have <u>a</u> ten-dollar bill. <u>Do</u> you <u>has</u> any smaller change?
        A   B   C

4. If you have no cash, you <u>can</u> charge <u>this</u> dinner <u>of</u> your credit card.
                         A   B   C

5. Alison <u>keeps</u> all her pennies <u>on</u> <u>a</u> piggybank.
        A   B C

6. Mrs. Larson <u>keep</u> her wallet <u>and</u> checkbook <u>in</u> her purse.
               A   B   C

7. I <u>has</u> quarters, dimes, nickels, <u>and</u> pennies in <u>a</u> coinpurse.
     A   B   C

8. Jackie tries to stick <u>to</u> a budget, <u>but</u> she always spends more money than
                        A   B

   she <u>shall</u>.
       C

9. When you <u>drops</u> the car payment off <u>at</u> the bank, get <u>a</u> receipt for it.
            A   B   C

10. At the end of <u>the</u> year, my taxes <u>amount</u> <u>of</u> thirty percent of my earnings.
                  A   B   C

> **MONEY EXPRESSIONS**
> 1. A fool and his money are soon parted. =
>   Foolish people spend their money foolishly.
> 2. My money is burning a hole in my pocket. =
>   I can't wait to spend my money.
> 3. Pocket money =
>   Change for small purchases
> 4. Stretch your dollar. =
>   Make your dollar buy more.

119

2. Read the following conversation and answer the questions.

> Anthony: I'm taking the bus into town for food.
> Kate: Be sure to take plenty of coins. You need exact change to ride the bus now.
> Anthony: Can you change a five-dollar bill for me?
> Kate: Let's see. Here are three ones, and a lot of change, but it's less than five dollars.
> Anthony: That's okay. I'll take it. I need the change.

1. Where is Anthony going?
   (A) To the bank
   (B) Into town
   (C) To work

2. Why does Anthony need lots of change?
   (A) To ride the bus
   (B) To pay for groceries
   (C) To change buses

3. How much money does Kate have?
   (A) Exactly $5
   (B) Less than $5
   (C) More than $5

4. What will Kate NOT do?
   (A) Take the bus
   (B) Give change to Anthony
   (C) Spend the $5

3. Read the following paragraph and answer the questions.

> People are using checks and credit cards for their daily purchases more and more. However, there are still times when only cash will do. Most vending machines will only accept cash. Parking meters only take change, and some only take quarters. Buses also require exact change.

1. What can checks and credit cards be used for?
   (A) Vending machines
   (B) Daily purchases
   (C) Buses

2. Only coins can be used for
   (A) parking meters
   (B) daily purchases
   (C) bank deposits

3. What is required for parking meters?
   (A) Checks
   (B) Credit cards
   (C) Coins

4. What requires exact change?
   (A) Buses
   (B) Trains
   (C) Planes

ANSWER KEY

1 Geography

Word Practice
1. Arctic Circle
   Equator
   Antarctic Circle
   South Pole
2. 2. rivers
   3. mountains
   4. oceans
   5. islands
   6. waterfalls
   7. mountain ranges
3. Water
   ocean
   river
   pond
   creek
   stream
   sea
   surf
   lake
   bay
   Land
   mountain
   hill
   shore
   valley
   peninsula
   plateau
   continent
4. 2. river bank
   3. plains
   4. pond
   5. coasts
   6. forest
   7. earth
   8. globes; maps
5. 1. East
   2. South
   3. Southwest
   4. Northwest

Reading Practice
1. 1. B flows
   2. B lies
   3. B is
   4. A is
   5. A is
   6. A are
   7. A of
   8. B they
   9. B of
   10. B has
2. 1. A   3. 1. A
   2. A   2. C
   3. B   3. B
   4. C   4. A

2 The Weather

Word Practice
1. dry - humid
   cold - hot
   clear - cloudy
2. thunderstorm
   windstorm
   snowstorm
3. 2. hot
   3. snow
   4. sun
   5. temperature
4. cloudy
   snowy
   stormy
   rainy
5. 2. windy
   3. snowy
   4. stormy/rainy
   5. breezy
   6. rainy
   7. icy
   8. sunny
6. 2. thunderstorm
   3. freezes
   4. Lightning
   5. temperature
   6. earth

Reading Practice
1. 1. C humid
   2. B were
   3. C in
   4. C high
   5. A no article
   6. B was
   7. A is
   8. A no article
   9. B of
   10. C no article
2. 1. B   3. 1. A
   2. A   2. B
   3. B   3. C
   4. A   4. C

3 The City

Word Practice
1. 2. street light
   3. stop sign
   4. street sign
   5. subway station
   6. bus stop
   7. telephone booth
   8. newspaper stand
2. 2. city hall
   3. movie theater
   4. apartment house
   5. concert hall
   6. museum
   7. opera house
   8. hospital
   9. hotel
3. 1. street
   2. road
   3. highway
   4. alley
   5. freeway
   6. lane
   7. drive
   8. boulevard
4. sidewalk
   curb
   crosswalk
5. parking meter
   parking lot

Reading Practice
1. 1. B to
   2. A crossed
   3. B and
   4. B park
   5. B go
   6. B to
   7. A come
   8. A on
   9. A Get
   10. C and
2. 1. A   3. 1. A
   2. B   2. C
   3. A   3. A
   4. A   4. B

4 Business

Word Practice
1. 2. operator
   3. typist / typewriter
   4. photocopier
   5. stapler
2. 2. calculator
   3. computer
   4. stapler
   5. photocopier
   6. word processor
3. 2. envelope
   3. receptionist
   4. pen
   5. staple
4. pen
   envelope
   paper
   pencil
   paper clip
5. telephone
   messages
   boss

6. stapler - attach
   file cabinet - file
   word processor - type
   wastepaper basket - throw away
   intercom - speak
   envelope - mail
7. 2. paper clip
   3. stapler

Reading Practice
1. 1. A on
   2. B uses
   3. A have
   4. C answer
   5. B in
   6. B and
   7. A orders
   8. C into/in
   9. C start
   10. B connect
2. 1. B   3. 1. B
   2. A   2. B
   3. B   3. C
   4. C   4. B

5 Types/B'ness

Word Practice
1. 2. bananas
   3. shoes
   4. lumber
   5. motor oil
   6. boats
   7. cushions
   8. stationery
   9. computers
   10. rubber band
2. 2. jeweler
   3. hair stylist
   4. grocer
   5. pharmacist
3. 2. luggage store
   3. department store
   4. drug store
   5. record store
4. 2. Yes, you can. At the toy store between the furniture store and the shoe store.
   3. Yes, you can. At the hair salon between the drug store and the candy store.
   4. Yes, you can. At the bike shop between the art gallery and the drug store.
   5. Yes, you can. At the furniture store between the dress shop and the toy store.
5. 2. compact discs
   3. chocolate bars
   4. racing bikes
   5. prescr. medicine
   6. sandals
   7. overnight bags

Reading Practice
1. 1. B opening
   2. B to
   3. C is
   4. B at
   5. A shopping
   6. C no article
   7. C go
   8. C no article
   9. C attract
   10. C to
2. 1. C   3. 1. C
   2. C   2. C
   3. A   3. A
   4. C   4. A

6 Restaurants

Word Practice
1. 2. reservation
   3. bartender
   4. lunch
   5. service
2. 1. breakfast
   2. lunch
   3. afternoon snack
   4. dinner
3. 2. high
   3. slow
   4. dirty
   5. smoky
4. 2. napkin
   3. glasses
   4. spoon
   5. plate
   6. fork
   7. knife
   8. saucer
   9. tablecloth
5. 2. soft drink
   3. waitress
   4. smoking section
   5. snack
   6. check
   7. tip
   8. silverware
6. 2. always
   3. sometimes
   4. never
   5. sometimes

Reading Practice
1. 1. A would
   2. C and
   3. A Put
   4. B she
   5. B will
   6. B for
   7. C and
   8. B use
   9. C their
   10. A is
2. 1. C   3. 1. B
   2. B   2. B
   3. C   3. C
   4. A   4. B

7 Office Terms

Word Practice
1. 2. office
   3. file cabinet
   4. envelope
   5. mistake
   6. desk
   7. clerical
   8. manager
2. file - file cabinet
   mistake - correction
   envelope - letter
   drawer - desk
   floppy disk - computer
3. Machines
   answering machine
   computer
   telephone
   word processor
   photocopier
   People
   boss
   secretary
   typist
   employee
   client
4. typographical mistake - typo
   facsimile - fax
   photocopy - copy
   memorandum - memo
   telephone - phone
5. Types
   memorandum
   fax
   letter

Ways to Prepare
word processor
electric typewriter
by hand
Ways to Send
mail
fax
by hand/courier
6. 2. pencil
   3. photocopy
   4. drawer
   5. mistakes

Reading Practice
1. 1. A store
   2. A became
   3. C to send
   4. A made
   5. C in
   6. A answers
   7. B for / from
   8. A is
   9. B puts
   10. B to hold
2. 1. B   3. 1. B
   2. B   2. C
   3. A   3. C
   4. A   4. A

8 Construction

Word Practice
1. to measure - ruler
   to cut - saw
   to drain - sink
   to screw - screwdriver
   to sand - sandpaper
   to turn on - power
2. toolbox
   saw
   hammer
   drill
   file
   nails
   screws
   ruler
   measure
   wood
   cuts
3. 2. hammering
   3. drilling
   4. sanding
   5. draining
   6. leaking
   7. dripping
   8. plugging
   9. turning on
   10. looking for
4. 2. leak
   3. fuse
   4. screwdriver
   5. sink
   6. measure
   7. work bench
   8. window
   9. wire
   10. saw
5. sandpaper
   toolbox
   workbench
   screwdriver
6. sink
   drain
   plumber
   plunger
   pipes

Reading Practice
1. 1. B on
   2. B used
   3. A connected
   4. B with
   5. B does
   6. A let
   7. A come
   8. B turn
   9. B fixed
   10. B in
2. 1. B   3. 1. A
   2. B   2. C
   3. C   3. B
   4. B   4. C

121

9 Entertainment

Word Practice
1. 2. director
   3. actor / actress
   4. performer
   5. singer
2. 2. television
   3. laughter
   4. music
   5. sit
3. concert
   symphony
   opera
   play
   musical
   movie
   comedy
4. classical
   symphony
   opera
   musical
   rock
5. 2. movie
   3. concert
   4. play
   5. conductor
   6. actress
6. Person
   audience
   cast
   chorus
   musician
   Action
   attend
   conduct
   direct
   perform
   Location
   balcony
   box
   cinema
7. 2. cast
   3. chorus
   4. row
   5. playhouse

Reading Practice
1. 1. B get
   2. B or
   3. B prefer
   4. C in
   5. A performing
   6. B of
   7. A perform
   8. B to eat
   9. A to use
   10. B for
2. 1. B   3. 1. B
   2. A   2. A
   3. C   3. B
   4. A   4. A

10 Teaching

Word Practice
1. math - arithmetic
   professor - teacher
   book - text
   learn - study
   subject - course
   correct - check
   test - examination
2. 2. studying
   3. learning
   4. majoring
   5. attending
   6. reviewing
   7. checking
   8. testing
3. 2. solve
   3. learn
   4. take
   5. fail
4. 2. laboratory
   3. history
   4. economy
   5. difficulty
5. 2. enrollment
   3. correction
   4. examination
6. 2. sophomore
   3. junior
   4. senior
7. 2. students
   3. bulletin board
   4. assignment
   5. course
   6. elementary
   7. seminar

Reading Practice
1. 1. C in
   2. B to pass
   3. B pass
   4. C and
   5. C to study
   6. B bring
   7. C in
   8. C and / while
   9. C fail
   10. C correct
2. 1. C   3. 1. B
   2. B   2. A
   3. A   3. B
   4. C   4. C

11 Medicine

Word Practice
1. hurt - ache
   medication-medicine
   physician - doctor
   sick - ill
   illness - disease
2. 2. dentist
   3. patients
   4. broken
   5. prescription
3. 2. medication
   3. operation
   4. injury
   5. treatment
   6. infection
4. Doctors
   x ray
   broken
   headache
   infection
   Dentists
   x ray
   broken
   tooth
   toothache
   infection
5. 2. operation
   3. cold
   4. ambulance
   5. broken
   6. x ray
   7. technician
6. patient
   hospital
   nurse
   medication
   pills
   injections
   x ray
   operation
   doctor
7. Person
   dentist
   nurse
   patient
   technician
   Condition
   fever
   headache
   infection
   sore
   Thing
   bandage
   medicine
   pharmacy

Reading Practice
1. 1. B and
   2. C to take
   3. B for
   4. B to save
   5. A removed
   6. C gave
   7. A and
   8. B to
   9. A stay
   10. B had

12 Hotel

Word Practice
1. 1. reserve
   2. register; check in
   3. check out
   4. tip; luggage
2. front desk
   check out
   room service
   double bed
3. 2. desk clerk
   3. check out
   4. double bed
   5. room service
4. 2. bellman
   3. doorman
   4. maid
   5. elevators
   6. lobby
   7. tip
   8. room service
5. reservations
   checked in
   clerk
   front desk
   registered
   key
   bellman
   luggage
   suite
6. Person
   doorman
   elevator operator
   guest
   maid
   Action
   register
   reserve
   Location
   front desk
   floor
   lobby
   lounge
   room
   suite
7. 1. 2   5. 5
   2. 3   6. 8
   3. 1   7. 6
   4. 4   8. 7

Reading Practice
1. 1. C asked
   2. B don't
   3. A would
   4. B need
   5. A and
   6. B while
   7. B in
   8. C and
   9. B and
   10. B ask
2. 1. A   3. 1. C
   2. C   2. B
   3. B   3. A
   4. C   4. B

13 Gardening

Word Practice
1. 2. hose
   3. rake
2. soil
   sprout
   water
   grow
   weeds
   vegetables
3. transplant - move
   bug - pest
   water - sprinkle
   pick - harvest
   grow - raise
4. 2. growing
   3. weeding
   4. planting
   5. watering
   6. harvesting
   7. sprouting
5. 2. harvesting
   3. watering
   4. sprouting
   5. spraying
   6. weeding
   7. planting

Reading Practice
1. 1. B require
   2. B to harvest
   3. A beginning
   4. A dig
   5. A ruined
   6. B to grow
   7. A is
   8. B and/before
   9. B rake
   10. C to grow
2. 1. B   3. 1. A
   2. C   2. A
   3. A   3. B
   4. A   4. C

14 Gas Station

Word Practice
1. 1. hood
   2. tires; air
   3. windshield
   4. gas tank; fill up
   5. trunk
2. 2. paper
   3. rain
   4. take a break
   5. oil
3. service station - gas station
   gas - fuel
   repair - fix a problem
   mechanic - car repairman
4. oil
   gas
   grease
   air
5. 2. change
   3. check
   4. pump
   5. repair
6. 2. changing
   3. check
   4. pumps
   5. repairing
7. 2. oil
   3. change
   4. hood
   5. trunk
8. 1. windshield
   2. hood
   3. tire
   4. trunk

Reading Practice
1. 1. B should
   2. C to fill
   3. C to change
   4. A checks the oil in her car once a week.
   5. A walks
   6. B can
   7. B to see
   8. A is
   9. A is
   10. B need to be replaced once a year.
2. 1. B   3. 1. B
   2. A   2. C
   3. B   3. B
   4. A   4. C

15 Military

Word Practice
1. 2. barracks
   3. submarine
   4. uniform
   5. troops
   6. drill
2. 2. duty
   3. uniform
   4. base
   5. combat
3. 1. flying
   2. drilling
   3. enlisting
   4. inspecting
   5. sailing
   6. marching
   7. recruiting
   8. joining
4. drill - practice
   base - "town"
   uniform - clothes
   combat - fighting
   barracks - dormitory
5. Person
   soldier
   officer
   Transportation
   tank
   Place
   camp
   barracks

Reading Practice
1. 1. B into
   2. C on
   3. C would
   4. B and
   5. B and
   6. C and
   7. B hopes
   8. B be
   9. C enlist
   10. A practices
2. 1. B   3. 1. C
   2. B   2. B
   3. A   3. A
   4. A   4. B

16 Police/ Law

Word Practice
1. violation - misdemeanor
   jail - prison
   patrol car - police car
   thief - robber
   attorney - lawyer
2. 2. criminal
   3. prosecutor
   4. judge
   5. thief
   6. prisoner
3. 2. sentenced
   3. booked
   4. arrested
   5. imprisoned
   6. judged
   7. witnessed
4. 2. witnesses
   3. judges
   4. sentences
   5. arrests
5. 2. testimony
   3. violation
   violator
   4. imprisonment
   5. prosecution
   prosecutor
   6. defense
   defender
   7. robbery
   robber

Reading Practice
1. 1. B with
   2. C worst
   3. C have
   4. C to testify
   5. B brought from
   6. B to wear
   7. C the longest
   8. B to grab
   9. C look for
   10. B will
2. 1. A   3. 1. A
   2. C   2. B
   3. B   3. B
   4. B   4. C

17 Artists

Word Practice
1. 2. chair
   3. lamp
   4. book
   5. television
   6. house
2. 2. palette
   3. tube
   4. still life
   5. landscape
3. 2. paint
   3. carve
   4. frame
   5. show
4. 2. showed
   3. framed
   4. painted
   5. carved
5. easel
   sketch
   paint
   oils
   watercolors
6. 2. collection
   collector
   3. painting
   painter
   4. sculpture
   sculptor

Reading Practice
1. 1. C on
   2. B known
   3. A painting/ to paint
   4. B go
   5. C to create
   6. C in
   7. B to use
   8. B go
   9. B of
   10. B to carve
2. 1. C   3. 1. A
   2. B   2. C
   3. A   3. A
   4. B   4. B

18 Banks

Word Practice
1. People
   teller
   bank manager
   customer
   Money
   service charge
   interest
   currency
   cash
   balance
   Form
   bank slip
   withdrawal slip
   checkbook
   deposit slip
2. 1. checking
   2. lending
   3. Banking
   4. cashing
   5. Withdrawing
   6. Borrowed
   7. credit cards
3. 1. 2
   2. $642.00
   3. $904.67
   4. $ 6.42
   5. $ 40.00
4. deposit
   withdrawal
   teller
   teller's window
   balance
   transaction
5. 1. J. Doe
   2. District Loan Co.
   3. Oct 5, 1991
   4. $55.00
   5. car loan payment
   6. 546

6. teller - customer
   deposit - withdrawal
   interest-service chg
   lend - borrow
7. 1. cashing
   2. lending
   3. withdrawing
   4. checking
   5. banking
   6. borrowing

Reading Practice
1. 1. C fill
   2. C cashing
   3. A to make
   4. B of
   5. B lend
   6. C on
   7. C to inquire
   8. B for
   9. A balancing
   10. A up
2. 1. C   3. 1. B
   2. A   2. C
   3. B   3. B
   4. C   4. C

19 Travel

Word Practice
1. 2. departure
   3. dining
   4. arrival
   5. reservation
   6. smoking
   7. driver
2. on time - late
   local - express
   smoking-non-
     smoking
   take off - land
   round trip-one way
   economy class -
     first class
3. 2. passport
   3. platform
   4. track
   5. customs
4. 2. lawyer
   3. station
   4. dining car
   5. coins
   6. luggage
5. Airplane
   flight
   jet
   pilot
   plane
   runway
   take off
   wing
   Train
   express
   platform
   train station
   Bus
   driver
   express
   platform
6. 2. air traffic controller
   3. reservation clerk/
     travel agent
   4. bus driver
   5. steward/
     stewardess/
     flight attendant

Reading Practice
1. 1. B go
   2. B to buy
   3. B is
   4. B stow
   5. A have
   6. C at
   7. A inform
   8. A smoke
   9. C cancelled
   10. B need
2. 1. B   3. 1. A
   2. A   2. A
   3. A   3. C
   4. B   4. B

20 Trains

Word Practice
1. 2. conductor
   3. passengers
   4. timetable
   5. track
2. ticket
   conductor
   ticket
   snack bar
   dining car
3. 2. travel
   3. reserve
   4. arrive
   5. board
4. Person
   conductor
   engineer
   passenger
   Action
   arrive
   board
   depart
   reserve
   Thing
   reservation
   ticket
   timetable
5. 2. express
   3. reserved
   4. snack bar
   5. luggage rack;
     seat
6. 2. fare
   3. schedule
   4. board
   5. gate
   6. seat
7. 2. departs
   3. reservation
   4. board

Reading Practice
8. 1. C eat
   2. A is
   3. C but
   4. C in
   5. A stay
   6. A depart
   7. A Look
   8. C depart
   9. C in
   10. C call
2. 1. C   3. 1. B
   2. B   2. C
   3. B   3. B
   4. A   4. A

21 Cars

Word Practice
1. 1. headlights
   2. windshield wipers
   3. tires
   4. wheels
   5. bumpers
   6. taillights
2. dashboard
   windshield
   taillight
3. 1. headlights
   2. brakes
   3. wheels
   4. seat belts
   5. seats
   6. bumpers
   7. windshield wipers
   8. taillights
   9. tires
   10. turn signals
4. 2. bumper
   3. wiper
   4. accelerator
   5. radiator
6. steering wheel
   windshield wiper
   passenger seat
   glove compartment
   turn signal

rearview mirror
gas tank
license plate
seat belt
6. Glove Compartment
   extra change
   pencil
   Trunk
   luggage
   spare tire
   jack

Reading Practice
1. 1. A careful
   2. C would
   3. C comfortable
   4. A fill
   5. C would
   6. B wear
   7. A on
   8. B conveniently
   9. C checked
   10. A on
2. 1. C   3. 1. A
   2. A   2. B
   3. B   3. B
   4. C   4. C

22 Roads

Word Practice
1. 2. throughway
   3. beltway
   4. freeway
   5. highway
2. 2. pass
   3. drive
   4. yield
   5. speed
   6. honk
3. speed
   highway
   pass
   signal
4. Vehicle
   van
   trailer
   truck
   motorcycle
   bus
   Action
   pass
   merge
   honk
   yield
   drive
   Location
   highway
   overpass
   lane
   median
   rest stop
5. toll
   turnpikes
   booths
   exits
6. 2. motorbike
   3. trailer
   4. truck
   5. van
7. 2. motorbike
   3. overpass
   4. motorcycle
   5. turnpike

Reading Practice
1. 1. B to get
   2. C to
   3. C pass
   4. C is
   5. C pull
   6. A on
   7. B get
   8. C pay
   9. B to drive
   10. B merge
2. 1. B   3. 1. A
   2. A   2. B
   3. B   3. B
   4. C   4. A

23 The Body

Word Practice
1. Right Side
   head
   neck
   chest
   arm
   hand
   knee
   ankle
   Left Side
   nose
   wrist
   elbow
   waist
   hip
   leg
   foot
2. 2. elbow
   3. palm; hand
   4. leg
   5. feet
   6. muscle
   7. lips
   8. shoulder
   9. stomach
   10. thumbs
   11. mouth
   12. tongue
   13. eyes
   14. cheek
   15. brain
   16. hand
   17. heart
   18. heart
   19. neck
   20. eye; eye
   21. head; toe
   22. back
3. 2. nose
   3. chin
   4. nails
   5. forehead
4. 2. thigh
   3. neck
   4. ankle
   5. eye
   6. wrist
   7. forehead
   8. throat
   9. head
   10. nail

Reading Practice
1. 1. B hurt
   2. C see
   3. B pumps
   4. B find
   5. B has
   6. B the
   7. B are
   8. C was
   9. C see
   10. C no article
2. 1. C   3. 1. B
   2. A   2. B
   3. B   3. C
   4. C   4. A

24 Clothes

Word Practice
1. 2. raincoat; umbrella
   3. shoelace
   4. belt
   5. sweater
   6. collar
   7. button
   8. skirt; purse
   9. jacket
   10. cuffs
2. raincoat - overcoat
   tennis shoes -
     sneakers
   pants - slacks
3. 2. jacket
   3. cuff
   4. skirt
   5. shoe

123

6. collar
7. suit/jacket
8. tie
9. shirt
10. pants
4. 2. slacks
3. shoes
4. gloves
5. trousers
6. socks
7. boots
5. Worn above
  shirt
  T-shirt
  sweater
  jacket
  Worn below
  boots
  shorts
  running shoes
  shoe laces
  tennis shoes
6. 1. on, put
   2. off, take
   3. away
7. 2. hat
   3. scarf; tie

Reading Practice
1. 1. B to be
   2. B and
   3. A get
   4. C is
   5. A wears
   6. A am
   7. C and
   8. B doesn't
   9. C are
   10. A to wear
2. 1. A   3. 1. B
   2. B   2. A
   3. C   3. C
   4. C   4. A

25 Housework

Word Practice
1. 2. dusting
   3. washing
   4. cleaning
   5. polishing
   6. ironing
2. 2. cleaning
   3. washing
   4. dusting
   5. Polishing
   6. ironing
   7. scrubbing
   8. mopping
3. sponge - rag
   soap - cleanser
   wash - clean
   sweep - vacuum
4. 2. cord
   3. sweep
   4. shower
   5. yard
5. 2. cleanser
   3. rug shampoo
   4. polish
   5. detergent
   6. ammonia
   7. bleach
   8. soap
6. 2. Bleach
   3. cleanser
   4. detergent
   5. polish
   6. soap
   7. water
   8. rug shampoo

Reading Practice
1. 1. A To sweep
   2. B and
   3. C try
   4. A was
   5. B scrubs
   6. C and
   7. B on
   8. A Pour
   9. C makes
   10. A clean

2. 1. A   3. 1. A
   2. A   2. C
   3. C   3. B
   4. A   4. B

26 Living Room

Word Practice
1. 2. woodwork
   3. mantel
   4. picture
   5. shelves
   6. painting
2. 2. shelves
   3. end tables
   4. drapes
   5. pictures
   6. chairs
3. 2. in
   3. to
   4. above
   5. under
   6. on
4. mantel
   shelf
   mirror
   painting
5. 2. of
   3. in front of
   4. behind
   5. across from
   6. in
   7. between
   8. beside
   9. next to
   10. in front of
6. 2. woodwork
   3. ashtray
   4. armchair
   5. bookcase
   6. fireplace

Reading Practice
1. 1. A in
   2. C is
   3. B and
   4. B has
   5. A on/over
   6. A and
   7. C matches
   8. B are
   9. C appears
   10. B allowing
2. 1. A   3. 1. B
   2. B   2. C
   3. C   3. A
   4. C   4. C

27 Kitchen

Word Practice
1. 2. toaster
   3. refrigerator
   4. coffee maker
   5. garbage disposal
2. glass
   spoon
   salt shaker
   cup
   napkin
3. 2. saucer
   3. sink
   4. cabinet
   5. tablecloth
   6. garbage
   7. placemat
   8. bowl
   9. broiler
   10. cup
4. 2. knife
   3. glass
   4. stove
   5. salt shaker
   6. dish
   7. bottle
   8. cabinet
   9. placemat
   10. napkin
5. 2. plant
   3. lamp
4. ceiling
5. seat
6. window
6. 2. fork
   3. pans
   4. pepper
7. 2. coffee maker
   3. garbage disposal
   4. oven
   5. toaster

Reading Practice
1. 1. A To set
   2. B and
   3. A have
   4. A her
   5. C no article
   6. A has
   7. A We
   8. C it
   9. B was
   10. C or
2. 1. C   3. 1. C
   2. B   2. B
   3. A   3. B
   4. C   4. C

28 Post Office

Word Practice
1. 2. letter
   3. stamp
   4. clerk; counter
   5. postmark
   6. parcel
   7. office box
   8. zip code
   9. label
   10. first class
2. 1. postage
   2. postal clerk
   3. postal code
   4. postcard
   5. post mark
   6. post office box
3. 1. I look in my mailbox.
   2. I see my mail.
   3. I open the envelope.
   4. I read the letter.
   5. I write a reply.
   6. I put my reply into an envelope.
   7. I seal and stamp my letter.
   8. I take it to the post office.
4. 2. weigh
   3. post office
   4. surface
   5. postmark
5. 2. address
   3. postmark
   4. stamp

Reading Practice
1. 1. C need
   2. C in
   3. B on
   4. B sold
   5. C was
   6. B sort
   7. A postmark
   8. A mail
   9. A was
   10. B label
2. 1. C   3. 1. C
   2. B   2. A
   3. A   3. C
   4. B   4. B

29 Food

Word Practice
1. Dairy Goods
   2. eggs
   3. cheese
   4. milk
   5. cream
   Baked Goods
   1. crackers
   2. cake
   3. cookies
   4. bread
   5. pie
2. 2. fish
   3. milk
   4. drive
   5. animal
3. bread - butter
   coffee - cream
   salt - pepper
   ice cream - cake
   tomatoes - lettuce
   oil - vinegar
4. 2. fish
   3. corn
   4. rice
   5. lettuce
   6. sugar
   7. cheese
   8. bacon
   9. milk
   10. pepper
5. 2. potatoes
   3. grapes
   4. beans
   5. onions
   6. cookies
6. 1. eggs
      flour
      milk
      sugar
   2. lettuce
      oil
      vinegar
      tomatoes
   3. bread
      butter
      lettuce
      chicken
      tomatoes
   4. meat
      salt
      pepper
      carrots
      onions

Reading Practice
1. 1. B found
   2. A is
   3. C for
   4. A eat
   5. C for
   6. A is
   7. B take
   8. A make
   9. C in
   10. C on
2. 1. A   3. 1. B
   2. C   2. C
   3. B   3. A
   4. A   4. B

30 Money

Word Practice
1. coins - change
   wallet - billfold
   money plan - budget
   cash - money
   dime - ten cents
   credit card - charge card
   one cent - penny
2. 2. charge
   3. pay
   4. earn
   5. save
3. 2. tax
   3. forget
   4. meal
   5. pen
4. 1. quarter; dime
   2. dimes; nickel
   3. quarters
   4. nickels; dimes
   5. quarters; pennies; dollar
5. 2. check
   3. receipt
   4. piggy bank
   5. taxes
   6. credit card
6. 2. credit card
   3. billfold
   4. payment
   5. budget

Reading Practice
1. 1. A keeps
   2. A would
   3. C have
   4. C to
   5. B in
   6. A keeps
   7. A have
   8. C should
   9. A drop
   10. C to
2. 1. B   3. 1. B
   2. A   2. A
   3. B   3. C
   4. A   4. A